# SoundBlaster™:
# Making WAVes
# with Multimedia

# Prima Computer Books

## Available Now!

1-2-3 for Windows: The Visual Learning Guide

Access 2.0 for Windows By Example (with 3 ″ disk)

ACT! 2.0 for Windows: The Visual Learning Guide

WINDOWS Magazine Presents- Access from the Ground Up

Build a Web Site: The Programmer's Guide

The CD-ROM Revolution

CompuServe Information Manager for Windows:
  The Complete Membership Kit & Handbook (with two 3 1/2″ disks)

Computer's Don't Byte

Computer Gamer's Survival Guide

CorelDRAW! 4 Revealed!

CorelDRAW! 4 for Windows By Example (with 3 1/2″ disk)

CorelDRAW! 5 Revealed!

Create Wealth with Quicken, Second Edition

Cruising America Online: The Visual Learning Guide

Excel 5 for Windows By Example (with 3 1/2″ disk)

Excel 5 for Windows: The Visual Learning Guide

Excel for the Mac: The Visual Learning Guide

Free Electronic Networks

Harvard Graphics for Windows: The Art of Presentation

IBM Smalltalk Programming for Windows & OS/2

Interactive Internet: The Insider's Guide to MUDs, MOOs, and IRC

Internet After Hours

Internet for Windows—America Online Edition:
  The Visual Learning Guide

KidWare: The Parent's Guide to Software for Children

Lotus Notes 3 Revealed!

LotusWorks 3: Everything You Need to Know

Mac Tips and Tricks

Macintosh Design to Production: The Definitive Guide

Making Movies with Your PC

Microsoft Office in Concert

Microsoft Office in Concert, Professional Edition

Microsoft Works for Windows By Example
OS/2 Warp: Easy Installation Guide
Migrating to Windows 95
PageMaker 5.0 for the Mac: Everything You Need to Know
PageMaker 5.0 for Windows: Everything You Need to Know
A Parent's Guide to Video Games
PC DOS 6.2: Everything You Need to Know
Procomm Plus for Windows: The Visual Learning Guide
PowerPoint: The Visual Learning Guide
Quicken for Windows: The Visual Learning Guide
Quicken 3 for Windows: The Visual Learning Guide
QuickTime: Making Movies with Your Macintosh, Second Edition
The Slightly Skewed Computer Dictionary
Software: What's Hot! What's Not!
Thom Duncan's Guide to NetWare Shareware (with 3 1/2" disk)
UnInstaller 3 Uncluttering Your PC
The Usenet Navigator Kit (with 3 1/2" disk)
Visual Basic for Applications Revealed!
The Warp Book: Your Definitive Guide to Installing and Using OS/2 v3
WinComm PRO: The Visual Learning Guide
Windows 3.1: The Visual Learning Guide
WinFax PRO 4: The Visual Learning Guide
Word 6 for the Mac: The Visual Learning Guide
Word for Windows 6: The Visual Learning Guide
WordPerfect 6 for DOS By Example
WordPerfect 6 for Windows: How Do I ...?
WordPerfect 6 for Windows: The Visual Learning Guide
WordPerfect 6.1 for Windows: The Visual Learning Guide

## How to Order:

For information on quantity discounts contact the publisher: Prima
Publishing, P.O. Box 1260BK, Rocklin, CA 95677-1260; (916) 632-4400. On
your letterhead include information concerning the intended use of the
books and the number of books you wish to purchase. For individual
orders, turn to the back of the book for more information.

# SoundBlaster™: Making WAVes with Multimedia

David Day
and
Valda Hilley

PRIMA PUBLISHING

Prima Publishing ™ and Design is a trademark of Prima Communications, Inc. Prima Computer Books is an imprint of Prima Publishing, Rocklin, California 95677.

Project Editor: Michael van Mantgem

Sound Blaster ™ is a trademark of Creative Labs, Inc..

If you have problems installing or running Sound Blaster 16, notify Creative Labs, Inc. at 1-(408) 428-6600.
Prima Publishing cannot provide software support.

Prima Publishing and the authors have attempted throughout this book to distinguish proprietary trademarks from descriptive terms by following the capitalization style used by the manufacturer.

Information contained in this book has been obtained by Prima Publishing from sources believed to be reliable. However, because of the possibility of human or mechanical error by our sources, Prima Publishing, or others, the Publisher does not guarantee the accuracy, adequacy, or completeness of any information and is not responsible for any errors or omissions or the results obtained from use of such information.

ISBN: 0-7615-0095-2
Library of Congress Catalog Card Number: 95-68044
Printed in the United States of America
95 96 97 98 AA 10 9 8 7 6 5 4 3 2 1

# Table of Contents

# Introduction

Congratulations: you're the proud owner of a Creative Labs Sound Blaster 16 audio card and perhaps a CD-ROM drive! This book is for you. You're in for some new audio treats that far surpass the tweedles and chirps you get from your PC's little speaker.

Even if you have the Creative Labs User manuals (and especially if you don't), I can help you get the best from your new equipment and its applications software.

You may have a multi-media PC with a Sound Blaster card, CD-ROM and applications software already installed. Jump right into Chapter 1 to connect audio and MIDI devices. Then keep reading to learn how to use the many Creative Labs applications to their best advantage.

Or, perhaps you bought a Sound Blaster setup–new or used–and need to install it. No problem: whether you've never even looked inside a PC before or are a technical whiz, I'll help you get your new purchase hooked up–and get the software installed. You'll be on the air before you know it!

Here's what you'll find inside:

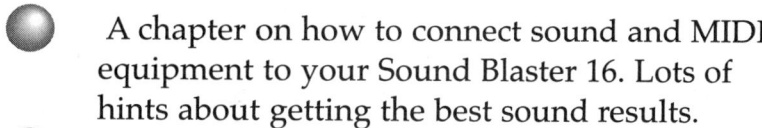 A chapter on how to connect sound and MIDI equipment to your Sound Blaster 16. Lots of hints about getting the best sound results.

Chapters showing how to understand and use each of the Sound Blaster Windows and DOS applications for sound record and playback and MIDI control.

An appendix showing you how to install the Sound Blaster 16 and CD-ROM drive.

Another appendix on how to install the Sound Blaster software applications.

# System Requirements

Here's the minimum kind of PC you should have to support the Sound Blaster 16 with CD-ROM drive (and my personal recommendations about what works best):

- IBM-compatible personal computer with 386SX or faster processor (486sx33 or faster is much better if you want good multi-media CD-ROM interaction)

- 4 Mb RAM (four megabytes of random access memory); 8 Mb RAM gives you noticeably faster Windows action

- 4 MB free disk space on your hard drive for the software; you'll want much more free space for Windows applications, sound and MIDI files

- MS-DOS 3.1 or higher; I suggest you upgrade to version 6.2 or newer for faster disk access

- Windows 3.1 (for Windows applications); I suggest you upgrade to Windows for Workgroups 3.11 even if you're not planning to use networks–it's faster and more reliable

- SVGA video (Super VGA video card with Windows-accelerated design, and compatible monitor, 640x480, 256 colors minimum, non-interlaced; monitor with 0.30mm dot pitch maximum)

- 3.5-inch, 1.44 MB floppy disk drive

- Mouse (two-button, Microsoft-compatible)

- One 16-bit expansion slot free for the Sound Blaster 16 card

- One 5.25in wide drive bay (half-height) free for the CD-ROM drive

You'll also need some speakers (or at least a pair of stereo headphones) to play the output from your Sound Blaster card. It's not required, but if you have an available stereo amplifier and full-sized speakers, you'll get far better sound.

# Sound Blaster 16 Specifications

Here is an extraction from Creative Labs' published specifications for your Sound Blaster 16 sound system (I have not verified these specs):

DIGITAL AUDIO

- Stereo and monophonic record and playback using 8-bit or 16-bit digital audio

- Industry-standard digital audio file formats

- Programmable sampling rates from 5Khz to 44.1khz

- Dynamic audio filtering and FIFO buffering

MIDI AUDIO and SYNTHESIZER

- Industry-standard MIDI files

- MPU-401 UART control (or Sound Blaster mode) with FIFO

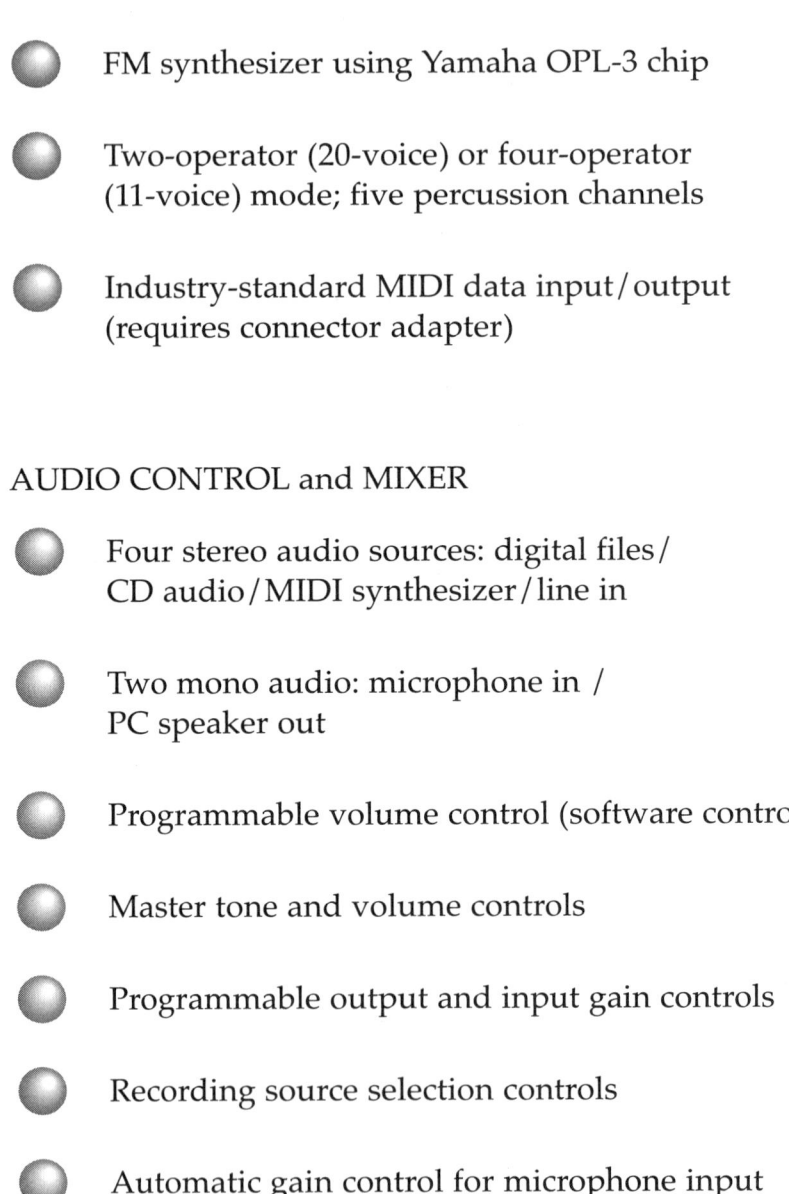

- FM synthesizer using Yamaha OPL-3 chip

- Two-operator (20-voice) or four-operator (11-voice) mode; five percussion channels

- Industry-standard MIDI data input/output (requires connector adapter)

AUDIO CONTROL and MIXER

- Four stereo audio sources: digital files/ CD audio/MIDI synthesizer/line in

- Two mono audio: microphone in / PC speaker out

- Programmable volume control (software control)

- Master tone and volume controls

- Programmable output and input gain controls

- Recording source selection controls

- Automatic gain control for microphone input

AUDIO OUTPUT

- Built-in stereo amplifier (4W / channel)

- Line level (preamplifier) output (may be jumper-selectable)

CD-ROM DRIVE (optional)

- Double-speed (300Kb / sec) max. transfer

- Access speed 320Ms average

- Storage on CD: 60Mb max

- Buffer memory 64Kb

- Audio output for headphone (front panel) or line (rear connector)

# What Went into This Book

Here are two systems we used successfully for the Sound Blaster 16 and its applications:

- An IBM-compatible PC with 486sx processor, 12Mb RAM, an S-VGA video card, 3.5-inch floppy drive and a Logitech mouse; MS-DOS 6.0 and Windows 3.1x

On this system, we installed a Creative Labs Digital Schoolhouse Bundle model MK4029 (to help make the kids happy). It included a Sound Blaster 16-bit audio card, a pair of Sound Blaster SBS30 speakers, and a Creative Labs double-speed CD-ROM drive model CR-563-B, made by Panasonic.

- An IBM-compatible PC with 486dx2-100 processor, 32Mb RAM, 540Mb hard disk, an ATI Mach 64 Windows-accelerated video card on a PCI bus driving an NEC MultiSync 5fgp monitor, 3.5-inch floppy drive, and a Logitech 3-button mouse; Windows 95. On this system, I used a Sound Blaster SB16 Value card, the Sound Blaster 16 Software on CD-ROM, and a Sony-made CD-ROM drive (using a separate controller). For sound output, I used an Altec-Lansing ACS300 self-powered speaker system with included sub-woofer.

- Microsoft Word for Windows 6.0 for writing the text and Quark for page-makeup

- SnapPRO! from Window Painters, Ltd., and Inset Systems HiJaak 4.0 for the screen shots

- US Robotics Sportster 28,800 V.34 modem, for transmitting files to the publisher (via CompuServe)

# Connecting Your Audio and MIDI Equipment

**Y**our new Sound Blaster 16 card has both audio inputs and outputs. They are designed to give you high-quality 16-bit ("CD-audio") sound. Here's how to make the right connections to get best performance from your new sound card.

All external audio connections to the Sound Blaster are on the board's handle; they're 1/8-inch ("mini") stereo audio jacks. Matching stereo plugs or cordsets are available at any Radio Shack. (The microphone input is a mono jack.) Here's how the handle connector lineup looks:

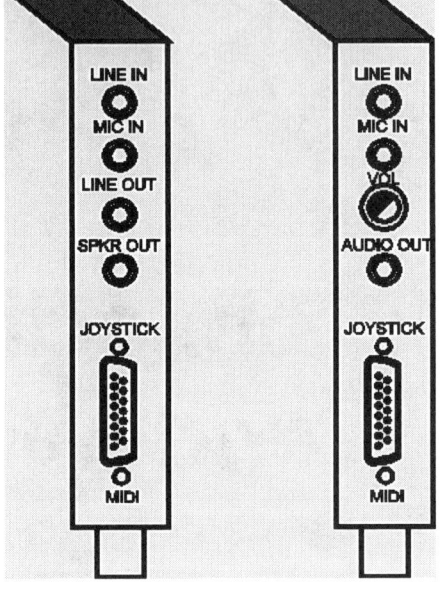

**Figure 1-1.**
Sound Blaster 16 handle and connectors

Sound Blaster 16 gives you five kinds of audio inputs:

● digital audio ("wave" files) from the on-board Sound Blaster D to A (digital-to-analog) converter

● instrument sounds from the on-board MIDI synthesizer

● a connection from the CD-ROM audio output to the Sound Blaster (for playing audio CD's)

● external **(LINE IN)** audio (from a preamplifier, tuner, external CD audio player, cassette player or music synthesizer for example)

● external **MIC IN** microphone input

Naturally, you can't "plug in" to the internal digital audio and MIDI inputs, or to the CD audio. CD audio goes directly from the CD-ROM drive to the Sound Blaster, via a cable inside your PC.

The Line In jack accepts a low-level high-impedance input from devices such as preamps, tuners or tape decks. If you use a little gadget called an "attenuator" (available at Radio Shack), you can also safely plug in outputs from speakers or other high-output devices to this input. Be sure to ask for advice before you do this!

Unlike some other sound boards, the microphone input the Sound Blaster provides is for a *dynamic* type microphone. Its specification is 600ohms impedance, at a -75db level. You can also use an "electret-type" microphone, that uses a built-in battery to power its self-contained preamplifier. Either of these microphone types is available at any good audio store; expect to pay from $5 to $50.

*Some sound boards use electrect microphones that require the sound card to provide electricity to power them. These will not work on the Sound Blaster.*

It's probably worth noting that the microphone input is the only one that's monophonic (single-channel); all the others are stereo.

Outputs on the Sound Blaster vary by the model; they include:

- **SPK OUT** connects to speakers or headphones. Output is 4 watts at 4ohms, 2 watts at 8ohms.

- **LINE OUT** is a low-level high-impedance output to a stereo amplifier, mixer, or tape recorder

- an internal output to drive the PC's internal speaker (this is optional, and not always used)

**SPK OUT** is a relatively low-power audio for speakers or headphones (but see the caution below). When this output is used at high level, the distortion can be very high (far beyond what's considered high fidelity). This is a great reason to use an external stereo amplifier and good quality speakers if you have them available.

The **LINE OUT** is in addition to the **SPK OUT.** Some versions of Sound Blaster don't have a separate **LINE OUT**. In that case, you can convert the **SPK OUT** on these versions to a low-level (line) output as I describe in Appendix A.

Sound Blaster versions that *don't* have **LINE OUT** may have a volume control in the same place, that you can use to set maximum speaker level. (You adjust it with a small screwdriver from the rear of the PC.)

*The Sound Blaster 16 built-in stereo amplifier has a maximum output power of four watts per channel with four-ohm speakers (two watts per channel if you use eight-ohm speakers). It's not much, but enough to blow out small speakers if you crank up the volume. For example, even the Creative Labs SBS30 Speakers sometimes bundled with the Sound Blaster aren't rated for this maximum output.*

*As with all audio sources, playing them at high volumes through headphones—especially for extended periods—can permanently damage your hearing!*

## Plugging in Your Audio Output Gadgets

There are several ways to enjoy sound from your Sound Blaster 16:

 Plug small speakers or headphones into the **SPK OUT** jack on the back of the audio card. Control the volume using the Creative Mixer application (described in Chapter 2).

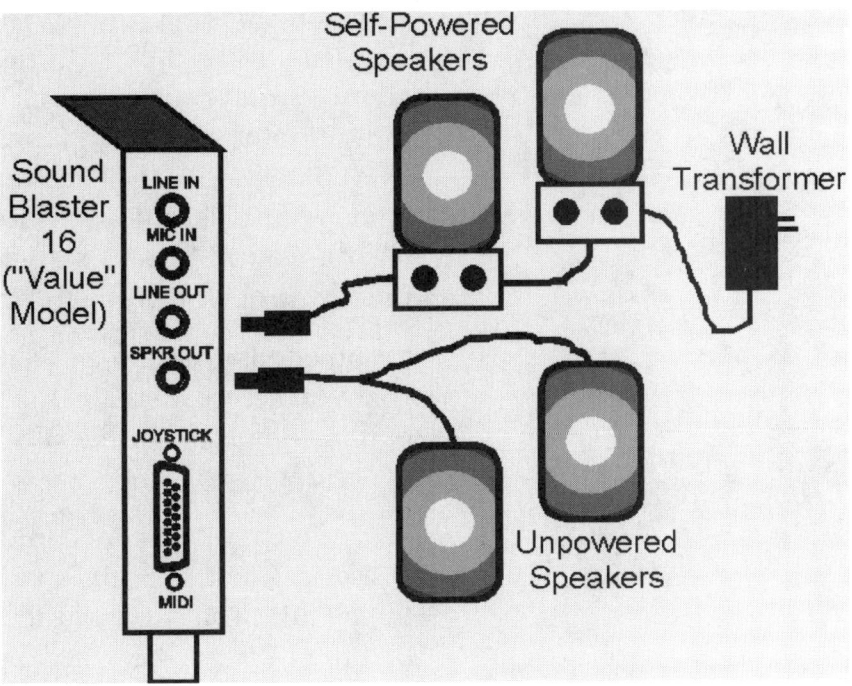

**Figure 1-2.**
Sound Blaster 16
output options

◉ Plug headphones into the Phones jack on the front plate of the CD-ROM player. Adjust the volume using the VOL knob next to the jack. Through this jack, you hear only the sound from the audio CDs you play on the CD-ROM. (This jack bypasses the Sound Blaster card completely.) There's not enough audio output to power speakers—unless you use self-powered speakers (see the next item below). Very limited use, but handy to listen to CD's without disturbing your cell-mates.

◉ Plug self-powered speakers into the Sound Blaster 16 card (or the CD-ROM headphone jack). You can find a wide variety of these speakers for sale, with self-contained audio amplifiers. Some are just toys, for $10 to $30 a pair; others give you startling fidelity, for $200 or more. They're powered by batteries or transformer adapters that plug in to ac. They may even have individual volume and tone controls on their front panels. Use these controls to adjust tone, balance, and set the maximum sound level. Then use the Sound Blaster's on-screen (software) volume controls for play settings.

If you choose battery-powered speakers, I suggest you set up a small trust fund to pay for the batteries; you could literally go through a set every day!

Self-powered speakers could plug into either the **SPK OUT** or **LINE OUT** jacks, depending on the circuit design. Read the instruction booklet before plugging them in, to get the best quality sound and avoid damage from overload.

 Plug an external stereo amplifier into the **LINE OUT** jack on the back of the card. (Use your existing full-sized stereo speakers already connected to the amplifier.) This approach gives you far more power, better tone and volume control, and both reduce distortion and improve frequency response. What's going to give you better sound: a pair of two-inch speakers powered by four watts, or your full-sized stereo system?

Finally, there's one connector on the Sound Blaster's handle with a double purpose:

 **Joystick/MIDI Connector** is a 15-pin jack that takes a PC-type joystick. Using an optional adapter, you can also attach MIDI-type musical instruments to the same connector. More on this on the following page.

## Joystick Connections

The joystick port on the Sound Blaster 16 works like any standard PC joystick input. The port is shipped ready to use; if it conflicts with a joystick port that's already installed in your PC, you must disable it. (See the side-bar headed "Jumper Joysticks" in Appendix A.)

## MIDI Connections

MIDI adds a whole new set of sound possibilities to your Sound Blaster. You can connect MIDI-equipped keyboards and external synthesizers, drum machines

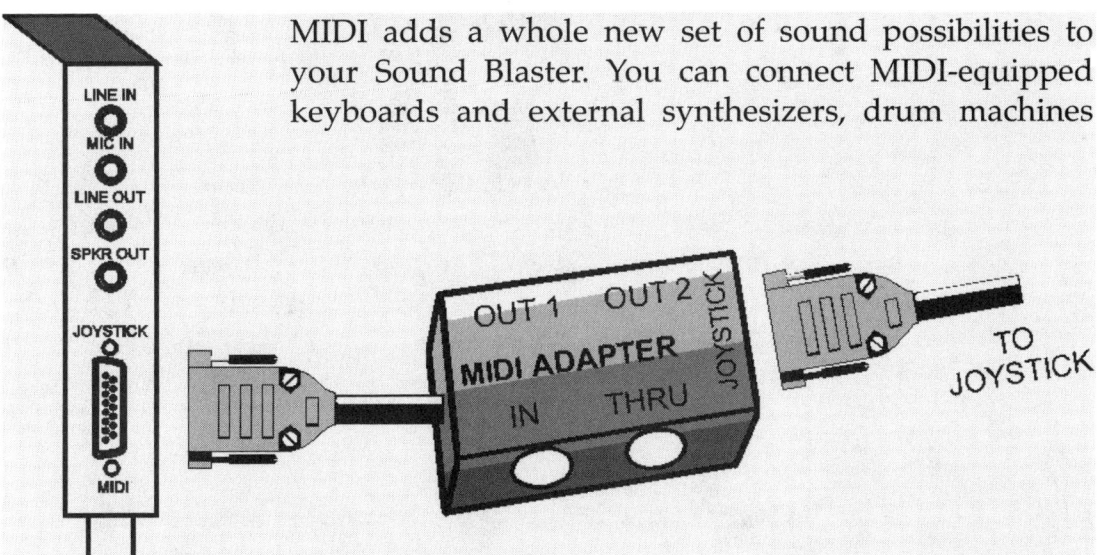

**Figure 1-3.**
MIDI adapter box example

and other MIDI devices. With available software, you can record, edit and play back your own musical creations. Or, you can buy or download, and then play pre-composed music in MIDI format. You can even find applications that teach you to play or understand music theory and composition.

If you want to add a MIDI instrument to your computer, you'll need a Sound Blaster MIDI kit or a compatible adapter from another manufacturer. This device is a small box with a cable that plugs into the **Joystick/MIDI** Connector. It's often available from PC retail stores for between $15 and $50. It provides MIDI IN, MIDI OUT and MIDI THRU connectors and a joystick connector as well. (You don't sacrifice your joystick connection when you add MIDI.)

MIDI devices communicate with each other—and with the Sound Blaster card—using special data signals. You connect between the devices using cables with round, 5-pin plugs. You'll need one cable to connect a device that generates MIDI signals (such as a keyboard) to the adapter box MIDI IN jack. You'll need another cable between the MIDI OUT jack and a device that generates musical sounds (called a "synth" or "module.") Sometimes a keyboard is used both to create and playback MIDI sounds (and needs two cables).

Instead of (or in addition to) an external MIDI sound generator, you can use the Sound Blaster 16's internal synthesizer to "play" MIDI music. This synthesizer is the Yamaha OPL-3 FM (frequency-modulation) chip. In effect, this chip converts the special MIDI file contents to audio signals that the Sound Blaster sends to its audio output.

## Internal Speaker Connection

Most computers come with a cheapo internal speaker to produce system alerts and sounds. It's driven by an even more cheapo circuit in your PC, and makes seriously low-quality sounds. You can substitute an output on the Sound Blaster 16 card to drive this speaker. This gives you somewhat better quality sound (obviously limited by the little internal speaker), and gives you control over volume levels. Because a few games will only send their sound effects through the PC speaker, using the Sound Blaster can perk them up.

If you want your Sound Blaster to control your PC's internal speaker, follow the simple connection instructions in Appendix A. (You'll need to open your PC to do this.)

*Before you begin using Sound Blaster, be sure your inputs are the proper kind and at the right level. An incorrect input could easily blow out Sound Blaster's input circuits. Also be sure your speakers are able to handle the volume levels you plan to use; small speakers are easy to blow out.*

*I suggest you start with all volume controls at their minimum settings, and slowly increase them until you have the sounds at your chosen listening level. You'll want to set volume levels using Creative Mixer, described in Chapter 3, or its DOS equivalent, in Chapter 6.*

*If you hear a loud hum or severe distortion at low volume levels, check again that the inputs are properly connected, and at the right signal level.*

Now, it's on for a close-up view of Creative Lab's software applications that give the Sound Blaster 16 power to record and play back audio and MIDI. One of them even gives it the power to speak. Read on, brave sound lover!

# 2

# Master Control and Audio Record and Play

n this chapter, I'll tell you about some of the Creative Labs sound applications for the Sound Blaster 16 that work under Microsoft Windows. These tools are fun and easy to use, and you'll find them easier after reading these pages.

If you have a pre-loaded multi-media PC, Windows is what you're sure to be using. If you have a DOS-based PC with at least a 486 processor and a VGA monitor, it's high time you installed Windows for Workgroups. (See my Introduction and Appendix B.)

If you have a less powerful computer, check out the DOS audio applications in Chapter 8. Some are graphical, and they give you many of the same features, but aren't nearly so slick.

When the Sound Blaster applications are installed in Windows, two program groups are created. Here's the Sound Blaster 16 group—the one with the main audio application icons:

**Figure 2-1.**
Windows Sound Blaster 16 group

Double-click the **EnsembleRemote** and the other three Ensemble icons and you'll have the "master" Sound Blaster application suite: Creative EnsembleAV, shown on page 13:

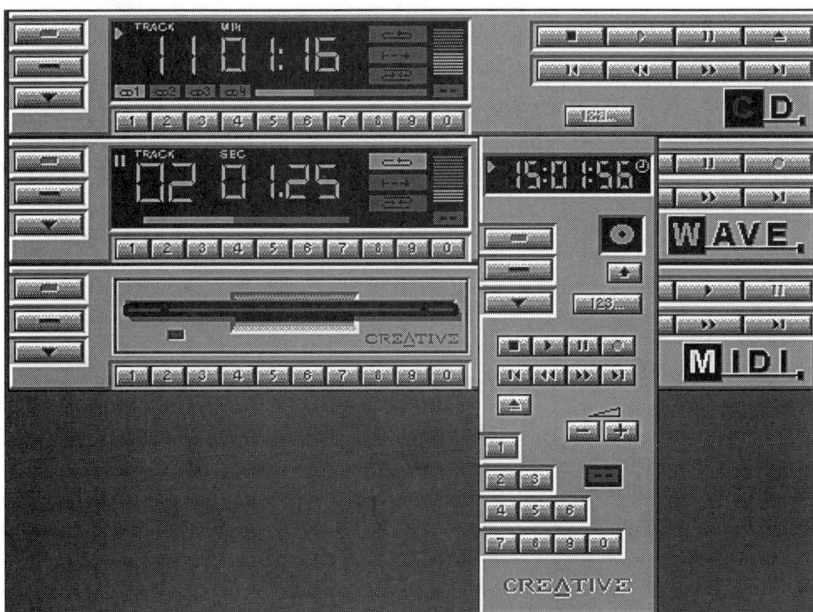

**Figure 2-2.**
Creative EnsembleAV
applications suite

Creative EnsembleAV on your Windows screen looks a lot like a stack of hi-fi components. That's really what it is: a set of four applications controlling your Sound Blaster's audio features. They are:

- **EnsembleRemote** looks and acts like a hi-fi remote control for the next three applications:

- **EnsembleCD**; plays your audio CDs on the CD-ROM drive.

- **EnsembleWave** records and plays back wave (.WAV) files. Wave files are actually digital audio recordings, stored as files on your hard disk. Windows plays them to give you those cute little sounds you can assign to actions (so you can hear things like Jean-Luc Picard ordering "Make it so" when Windows opens). Using a microphone, or any other audio source, you can record your own!

**EnsembleMIDI** plays back MIDI (.MID) files through the music synthesizer on your Sound Blaster 16. The big advantage of MIDI is that a very small file can create lots of music. More on MIDI a bit later.

# EnsembleRemote

This is one remote control that won't get lost under the couch cushions—or on your computer display. EnsembleRemote lets you control the EnsembleCD, EnsembleWave, or EnsembleMIDI audio applications. Its front-panel buttons control your choice of one of these at a time.

## Using EnsembleRemote

EnsembleRemote pops up at a mouse click and looks like this:

**Figure 2-3.**
EnsembleRemote
control panel

The EnsembleRemote controls are a lot like those on a regular stereo remote. This on-screen panel lets you select between CD audio, digital audio on disk files or MIDI. Once you've selected the audio source, you can select the track, and play, record, fast forward and reverse.

What you're listening to appears in bright blue-green "luminescent" style letters in a display window. You have your choice of several display indications. Other buttons give you power off and volume control.

The power of Windows gives you features you won't get from Sony: a pull-down menu for more controls and a minimize button to make the remote shrink to an icon (or for Windows 95, to a button on the Taskbar). You can either use the mouse to control these applications, or use keyboard commands (which I'll list for you later). You can also click on any on-screen application and drag it wherever you want.

Let's take a look at some of these features. First, a quick tour of the control panel. Here's a view of the overall layout:

At top is the "touch-sensitive" display.

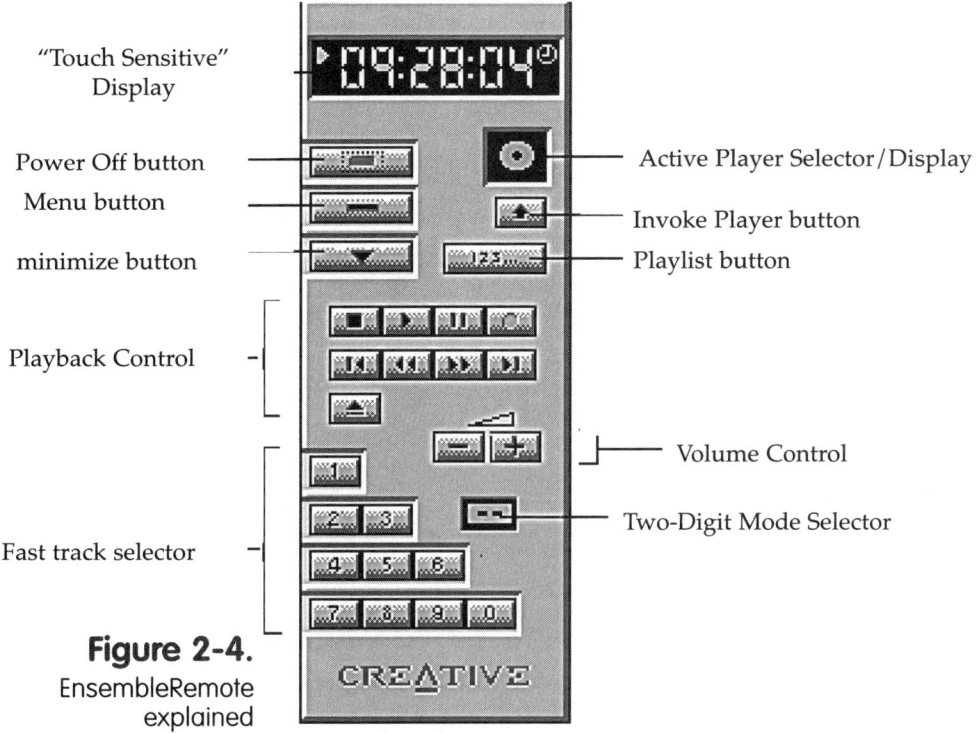

"Touch Sensitive" Display

Power Off button

Menu button

minimize button

Playback Control

Fast track selector

Active Player Selector/Display

Invoke Player button

Playlist button

Volume Control

Two-Digit Mode Selector

**Figure 2-4.**
EnsembleRemote explained

The main control buttons, to turn the application off, to minimize it and to display the menu, are at top left. To the right of those are the buttons to select one of the three active players and to display the "playlist"—list of sounds being played.

In the center are the familar transport controls to play, record, pause, fast-forward and rewind. In that same group is a button to eject the CD (to open the door). To the right of that are two digital volume controls ("+") and ("-").

Finally, at the bottom, is a cluster of number buttons to select the track you want to hear. At the right is a "mode selector" button, to let you enter either one or two track digits (if you have lots of tracks).

Now, let's get some closeup views.

## Changing the display contents

Here's a detailed look at the EnsembleRemote display:

**Figure 2-5.**
Ensemble "touch-sensitive" display window

Using a "touch" (make that a click) from a mouse pointer, anywhere in the display window to cycle between showing:

- The time, according to your PC clock (not chronometer-accurate, but probably as good as your VCR)

- The title of your playlist, if you assigned one (more on that later)

- The number of the current track, or the track title (if you assigned one on the playlist)

## Select the active device

The active device is the player you're currently controlling with the EnsembleRemote. Choose the device by clicking on its individual icon (see Figure 2-1). Quicker yet, simply click on the small arrow button below the Active Device icon (called out in Figure 2-4). When you do, the player selection group pops out, as shown here:

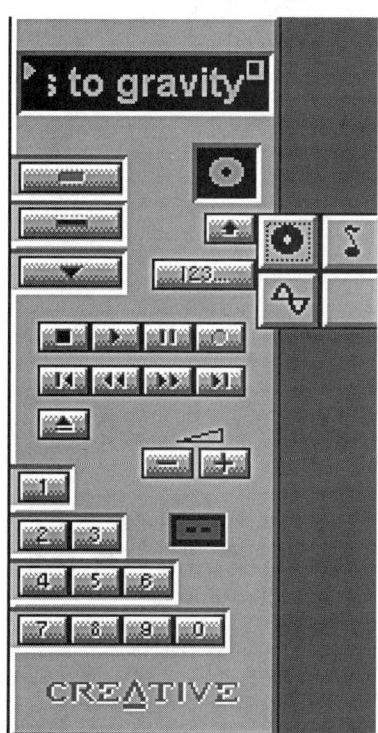

**Figure 2-6.**
EnsembleRemote
transport selection
buttons.

You can now see the three active device icons: EnsembleMIDI, EnsembleWave, and EnsembleCD. The CD icon looks like a CD disk, the Wave (digital audio) player looks like an oscilloscope wave, and the MIDI player has a note symbol.

Click on a symbol, the player application appears and the active transport icon changes to the same symbol.

## Power Off, Menu and Minimize buttons

These buttons are in a vertical group at left in figure 2-7:

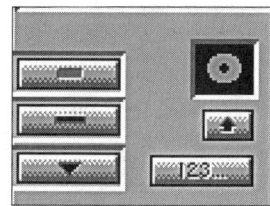

**Figure 2-7.**
Power Off / Menu /
Minimize buttons

The Power button closes EnsembleRemote, which disappears from your screen. This button only works for "off" of course, because EnsembleRemote must be "on" for you to see the button. If you want the application back, go to the Sound Blaster 16 group (or folder) and double-click on its icon once again.

If you have one or more transport deck applets active on your screen, they will remain active until you click them off separately.

When you click on the Menu button, a menu drops down in front of EnsembleRemote:

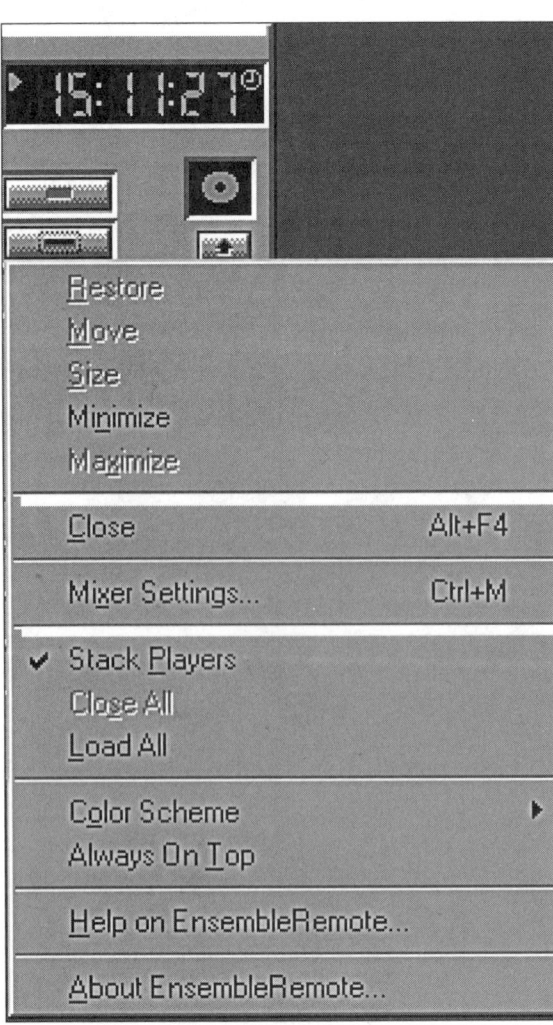

**Figure 2-8.**
EnsembleRemote's
drop-down menu

If you select Always on Top from the menu, that forces EnsembleRemote to always be in view above your other active Windows applications. For example, you might want it to select some soothing audio CD tunes while figuring out your taxes using Excel or Quicken.

Another handy tool you'll find here is Creative Mixer, which lets you control the volume and balance for every audio device controlled by the Sound Blaster. Click on **Mixer**, and you'll see:

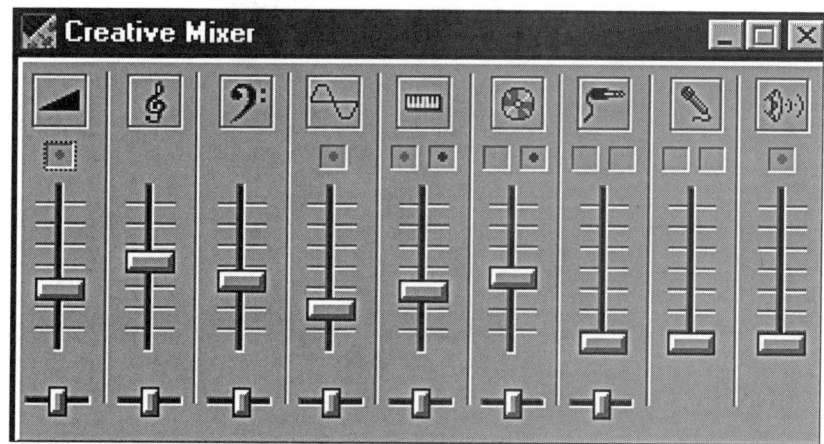

**Figure 2-9.**
Sound Blaster 16's
Creative Mixer applet

Creative Mixer even has its icon in the Sound Blaster 16 program group; you can also click there to bring it up.

Each sound device has its own slide volume control, identified by an icon, and there's a master control as well. Use your mouse to slide a control up and down to select the volume. Small sliders at the bottom of each control (for stereo sources) move right and left to adjust balance. You'll also see little red and green dots that you can click to enable or disable each source for record and playback. (I'll leave it to your imagination which color is which.)

I'll discuss Creative Mixer in a little more detail in the next chapter.

Finally, the Minimize button, in this little group of three, reduces EnsembleRemote to an icon; which is neatly parked at the bottom of your Windows screen. (If you're lucky enough to be using Windows 95, it will become a button parked on your Taskbar, at the bottom edge of your display.)

## Select and setup the play list

An extremely handy and fun-to-use feature is the play list. If you pop in an audio CD in your CD-ROM, it's logged in to EnsembleRemote by its own digital serial number. In the future when you play the CD, it's automatically identified. All you have to do is type in the name of the CD, and the names of each tune, and they're stored and recalled each time as well. Here's how.

Select the CD player, using the player selection button. Put in an audio CD, and click on the playlist button. Here's what drops in front of EnsembleRemote:

**Figure 2-10.**
EnsembleRemote
play list box

This shows a volume called *Sonata Brutalle* by Thanks to Gravity (an alternative rock group). I've already entered the title of the CD at top, and all its tracks (cuts) in the list at right.

At left, is the list in the order I want the tracks played. All I had to do was click on a song using the *right* mouse button, drag it to the new position, and release. Next time you play your CD's, have it your way! (What other way to put *fourth* place in second place?)

Minutes later, I loaded another CD (piano music by Erik Satie), and EnsembleRemote dutifully recalled its play list.

This table gives you a more complete explanation of the dialog box buttons and lists:

| Dialog Block | Content |
|---|---|
| CD Artist/Title | Name of your CD. At first, it comes up with "No Title." You can change that to the real title (like "Thanks to Gravity"), or any name you choose) |
| Track Title | Name of each track. Until you enter the actual names, only the track numbers are shown here. |
| Playlist | Names of all tracks you included in the playlist |
| Track List | Names of all tracks on the CD |
| Play | Command to play the tracks from the Playlist or Track List |
| Add | Command to add selected tracks from the Track List to the Playlist |
| Add All | Command to add all titles on the Track List to the Playlist |
| Clear | Command to clear all track names from the Playlist |
| Remove | Command to remove any currently selected names from the Playlist |
| Done | Command to accept tracks selected for the Playlist |
| Cancel | Command to reject changes made to the playlist |
| Help | On-line help system |

You can make up similar play lists for MIDI or Wave (digital audio) collections. In this case, you'll be asked for a collection title to catalog (since there's no physical tape or CD disk, EnsembleRemote can associate with sounds for these applications).

# Transport control buttons.

These buttons are just like the ones on your hi-fi or VCR deck at home. They control the deck currently selected as the active player. The top row, from left-to-right, is:

stop/forward/pause/record

and the bottom row is:

rewind/fast-reverse/fast-forward/end

Piece of cake (but here's a picture anyway):

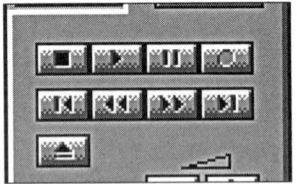

**Figure 2-11.**
EnsembleRemote transport controls

# CD eject and volume controls

Next down are two controls that control the CD deck and volume. Click on the eject button at left, and the CD transport opens, to let you put in a disk. Click again, and the drawer closes.

Click on the "+" and "-" buttons at right to adjust the volume for the active deck. (This has the same effect as the "master" volume in the mixer applet.) Here's how these incredibly complex controls look:

**Figure 2-12.**
EnsembleRemote eject and volume control

## Track and Mode buttons

Want to jump to a particular numbered track on your CD or cut on your Wave or MIDI playlist? Just click on one of the numbered buttons. (Button "0" selects track 10). Here's how they look:

**Figure 2-13.**
EnsembleRemote
Track and Mode
buttons

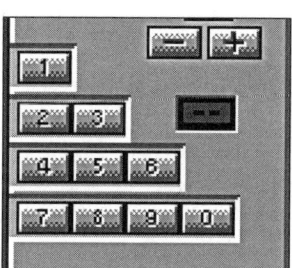

What, you want more than 10 tracks? Click once on the "mode select" button at right to highlight it. Now you can enter two digits on the number buttons. (Not only that, you must enter two digits; there's no timeout for just one. For example, if you now want track 5, you must enter a "0" and then a "5".)

## Keyboard Shortcuts for EnsembleRemote

If you are mouse-challenged, or the mouse isn't working because the kids dropped it in the fishbowl, relax. You can use keystrokes on the keyboard instead. For this to work, EnsembleRemote must be the application in *focus* (it must be the one that's selected on your Windows desktop).

Table 2-1 on page 24 shows you the keyboard characters that control all functions of EnsembleRemote:

**Table 2-1.** Keyboard Commands for EnsembleRemote

| KEY | ACTION |
|---|---|
| A | Pause track/sound file |
| B | Play previous track/sound file |
| C | Activate Select Device icons |
| Ctrl - D | Change the "touch-sensitive" display |
| D | Lower the volume |
| E | Load or eject the CD player |
| F | Play next track/sound file |
| F | Show on-line Help |
| H | Activate the Select Device button |
| K | Rewind track/sound file |
| L | Open selected playlist |
| N | Minimize EnsembleRemote to its icon |
| O | Exit EnsembleRemote |
| P | Play track/sound file |
| S | Stop track/sound file |
| Spacebar | Accept selection |
| T | Activate 2-digit mode |
| U | Turn up volume |
| W | Fast-forward track/sound file |
| 0 - 9 | Select track/sound file |

Now it's time for a closer look at the three separate audio "deck" applications that EnsembleRemote controls. Here's how they look all stacked together:

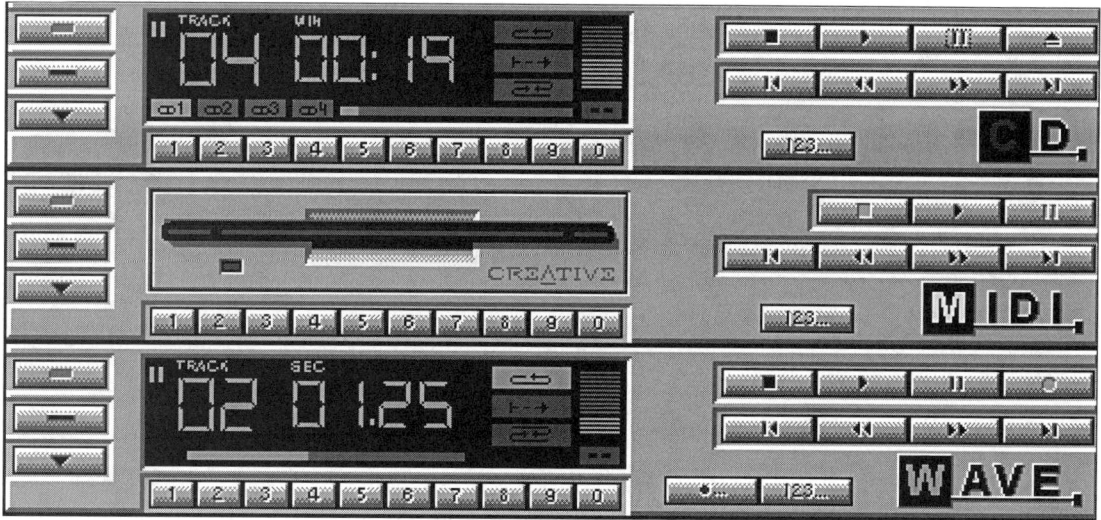

**Figure 2-14.**
EnsembleAV
transport stack

# EnsembleCD

EnsembleCD turns your expensive computer into something really useful: a stereo to play audio CDs! Ain't technology grand? And, you can build a playlist to change the order of songs or skip the ones you can't stand. EnsembleCD also lets you name the tracks on your CD collection.

## Starting EnsembleCD

To run EnsembleCD, simply double-click on its icon (above) in the Sound Blaster 16 group window. Or you can bring up the CD transport by clicking on the CD-disk shaped icon from the EnsembleRemote device select icons. Figure 2-8 shows the EnsembleCD application ready to use:

Power Off button  "Touch Sensitive" Display  Playback Control

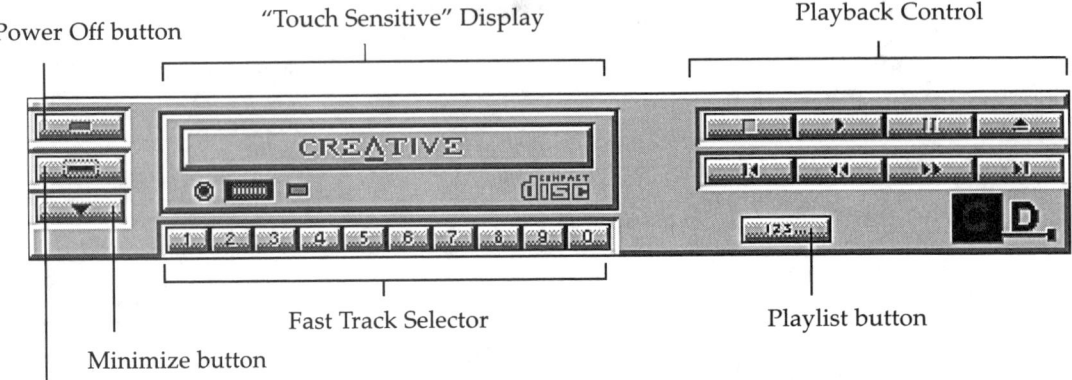

Fast Track Selector  Playlist button

Minimize button

Menu button

**Figure 2-15.** EnsembleCD—a graphical CD player

# Selecting indications in the "touch-sensitive" display

The "touch-sensitive" display has three different contents to choose from. Click with your mouse anywhere in the window area to switch between them. Here's how all three displays look:

**Figure 2-16.** EnsembleCD display choices

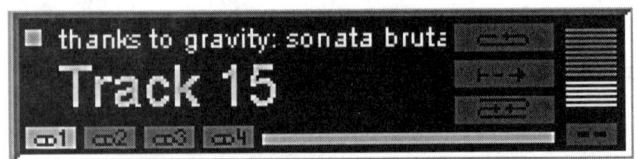

And here's what's going on in each of them:

● **CD-ROM drive**, with a green light to indicate that a CD is in the drive; when you eject the CD, the graphics "door" obligingly "opens" in response. (It's interesting to note that you can open and close the CD drawer with a button on EnsembleRemote, but there's no button for that on EnsembleCD itself.)

● **CD and track titles**, showing the name you have cataloged for each CD and its tracks

● **Track number and length**. The digital readout, with the information fields labeled. "Length of Track" tells how much time remains for the track being played.

Just to the right of the digital display is a set of three play mode icons: Repeat Mode replays the playlist when the last cut finishes playing; Introduction Mode plays the first few seconds of each track in the playlist; Shuffle plays tracks from the playlist in no particular order at all. Very adventurous, yes?

To the far right in the display window is a vertical-bar type volume control that shows your CD's current volume setting. You can also drag this bar up and down to control volume.

EnsembleCD can control up to four CD drives, if you have the money and room to install them on your system. The tiny icons in the bottom of the window are marked CD1, CD2, CD3, and CD4; click on one to light it and select the active drive.

Just to the right of the CD icons is a lighted bar that represents how much of the track has been played. You can even drag the lit bar with the mouse right or left to move ahead or back in the track's play position.

## Track selection

Below the display is a row of track selection buttons, like those for EnsembleRemote. If you have *more than* 10 tracks, choose two-digit mode by clicking on the button on the bottom right of the display (just below the vertical volume control).

## EnsembleCD Menu Commands

Press the menu button to see the EnsembleCD drop-down menu. Like EnsembleRemote, it has choices to either close the application, or to select on-line help. Unlike EnsembleRemote, it cannot be made to stay on top of other Windows applications.

## Playlist button

Playlist lets you pick the tracks (songs) you want to play from a single CD. Click on the Playlist button (the one with "123" on it), and you get the same CD Playlist dialog box you saw for EnsembleRemote in Figure 2-8 on page 18.

## Playback Buttons

EnsembleCD has a set of transport control buttons, that work just like your home stereo remote control (and just like the set I showed you for EnsembleRemote in Figure 2-11 on page 22).

## Keyboard Shortcuts for EnsembleCD

If you prefer, you can use the keyboard to access all functions for EnsembleCD; here's the list:

**Table 2-2.** Keyboard Commands for EnsembleCD

| Key | Action |
| --- | --- |
| A | Pause track |
| B | Play previous track |
| Ctrl - D | Change the "touch-sensitive" display |
| E | Load or eject the CD-player |
| F | Play next track |
| F1 | Show on-line Help |
| G | Activate the Graphic Sound Control |
| H | Activate Shuffle (random playback |
| I | Start Introduction mode (sample playback) |
| K | Rewind track. |
| L | Open Playlist dialog box |
| M | Repeat mode |
| N | Minimize EnsembleCD to its icon |
| O | Exit EnsembleCD |
| P | Play current track |
| S | Stop playing track |
| Spacebar | Accept selection |
| T | Activate 2-digit mode |
| W | Fast-forward track |
| 0 - 9 | Select track/sound file |

# EnsembleWave

EnsembleWave is a digital record/playback application. Instead of recording on tape, it uses files on your hard disk in a special digital audio format called WAVE. These files have the letters WAV at their end; for example, TEST.WAV.

You can record from the microphone, or from an audio CD or the included MIDI synthesizer, and also from any external audio you plug into the line input jack.

## Starting EnsembleWave

To use this program, double-click on the EnsembleWave icon in the Sound Blaster 16 group window. Or, you can select the "oscilloscope" button on EnsembleRemote. The EnsembleWave controller appears (see Figure 2-17).

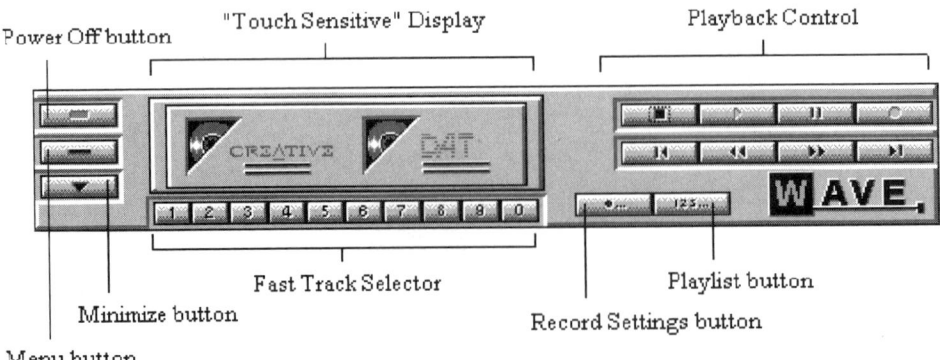

Power Off button    "Touch Sensitive" Display    Playback Control

Minimize button    Fast Track Selector    Playlist button

Menu button    Record Settings button

**Figure 2-17.**
The EnsembleWave control panel

# Changing the "Touch-Sensitive" Display

This panel looks almost like EnsembleCD, except it has a record button. (It's hard to make a recording on a CD— at least with today's home PC technology!)

The "touch-sensitive" display has three different faces to choose from; it's almost identical to the display for EnsembleCD. Here's what you'll see in each of the three displays:

**Figure 2-18.**

EnsembleWave display panel

A "tape deck" door, that looks a lot like a cassette tape deck. The door "closes" whenever a WAVE file is playing, and "open" when it's done. (No "door" appears when you're recording files; you can choose instead between the next two displays.)

The currently selected WAVE file number and elapsed time for the file.

Title of the current WAVE file and playlist group; if you're recording (as shown here), it also tells you the digital format you've chosen for this file.

For details of the display contents and buttons, refer to the EnsembleCD display in Figure 2-16; the WAVE transport is almost identical to the CD one (except that it also shows Recording status).

# Recording a Wave File

What's so exciting about a WAVE transport? You can "roll your own" sounds: record and edit anything that fits your fancy. Using the Sound Blaster editing tools, you can combine and modify sounds for all kinds of special effects. You can even "clip" voices and sounds from external sound sources. Use your favorite creations to replace the WAVE files that Windows uses to announce various events.

You can record WAVE files in mono or stereo, and in several quality levels, depending on the number of bits per sample and the sample speed. The slowest and smallest samples have audio quality like a telephone, and the fast, big ones sound nearly as good as an audio CD. The better the sound, the more space it takes on your hard disk; stereo (two channels) doubles the space needed.

(If you decide to make high-quality WAVE files, you may be limited to rather short recordings. That's because they chew up enormous amounts of hard disk space. For example, at the best quality stereo setting, you'll use more than 10 megabytes of disk every minute!)

So let's make some music! To create your own WAVE (.WAV) files, follow these steps:

1   Click on the EnsembleWave Menu button.

2   Select CD Sync or MIDI Sync from the menu options. (When you later press the EnsembleWave Record button, the CD player will automatically start.)

3   Select the Mixer, and adjust the play level for the CD and record level for the WAVE application.

4   Click on the Record button.

5   The WAVE recording format dialog appears:

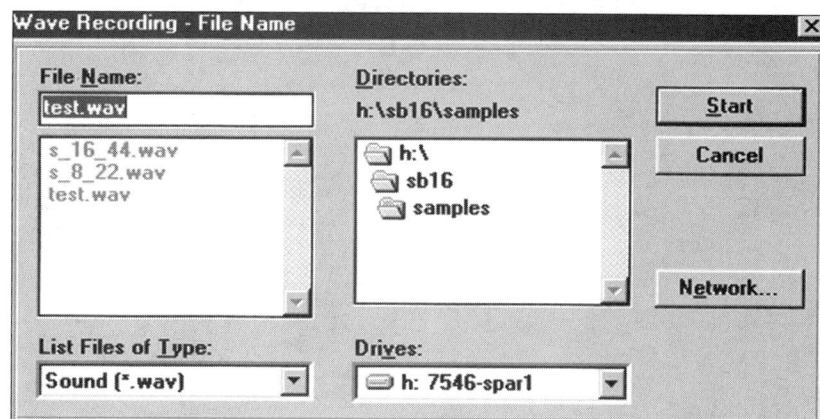

**Figure 2-19.**
EnsembleWave
recording format
dialog

**6** Select the recording format you want. The 8-bit, 11Khz mono recording is the lowest quality, and gives you the smallest files. The 16-bit, 44Khz stereo format takes 16 times as much file space.

When you click on OK, the Wave Recording dialog appears:

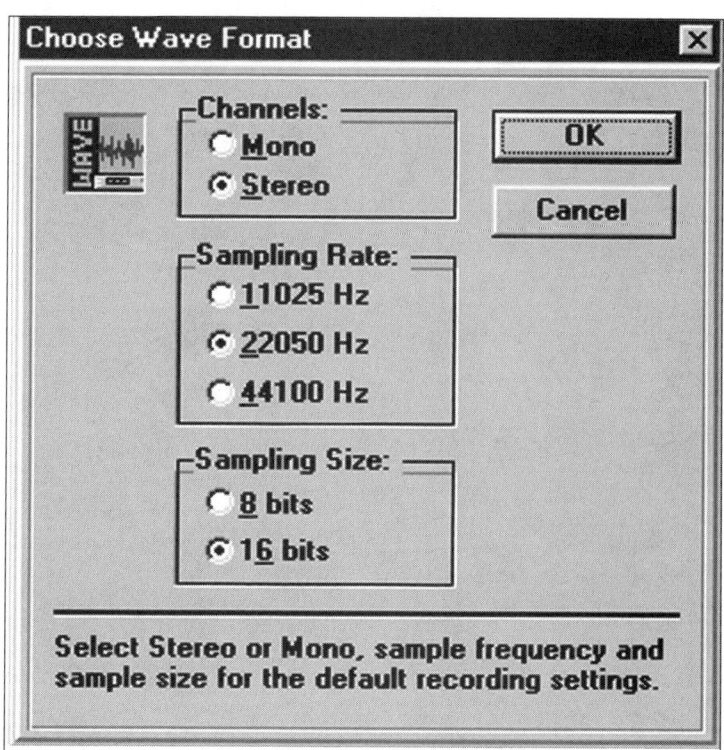

**Figure 2-20.**
The EnsembleWave
Wave Recording
dialog

**7** Type the name of the new wave file in the File Name box. In the sample, you see the filename "test.wav". Pretty boring, eh?

**8** Select the directory and the drive where you want to save the file. This SAMPLE directory is one the Sound Blaster installation created.

**9** Press Start to begin recording (See sidebar, "From CD to Wave"). The CD begins playing and the WAVE file begins recording.

## FROM CD TO WAVE

Before pressing that Start button on EnsembleWave, go to EnsembleCD and choose an audio cut you want to record as a wave file. If you want only a piece of a song, use the Graphic Slider to move to the starting position you want.

When you have the CD set where you want it, click on the Pause button on EnsembleCD. That's all there is to it.

Once you have the CD player set up, press EnsembleWave's Start button. This also activates the CD player from your paused position. When your recording is finished, click on the Stop button on the EnsembleWave control panel.

(You could have just as easily chosen the MIDI transport instead of the CD one.)

## Playing Wave Files from the Playlist

A playlist is a group of files you put together to play back in a set order.

## Building or Editing a Playlist

To build or playback a playlist of wave files, follow these steps:

**1** Click EnsembleWave's Playlist button.

**2** The Wave Playlist dialog opens (see Figure 2-21).

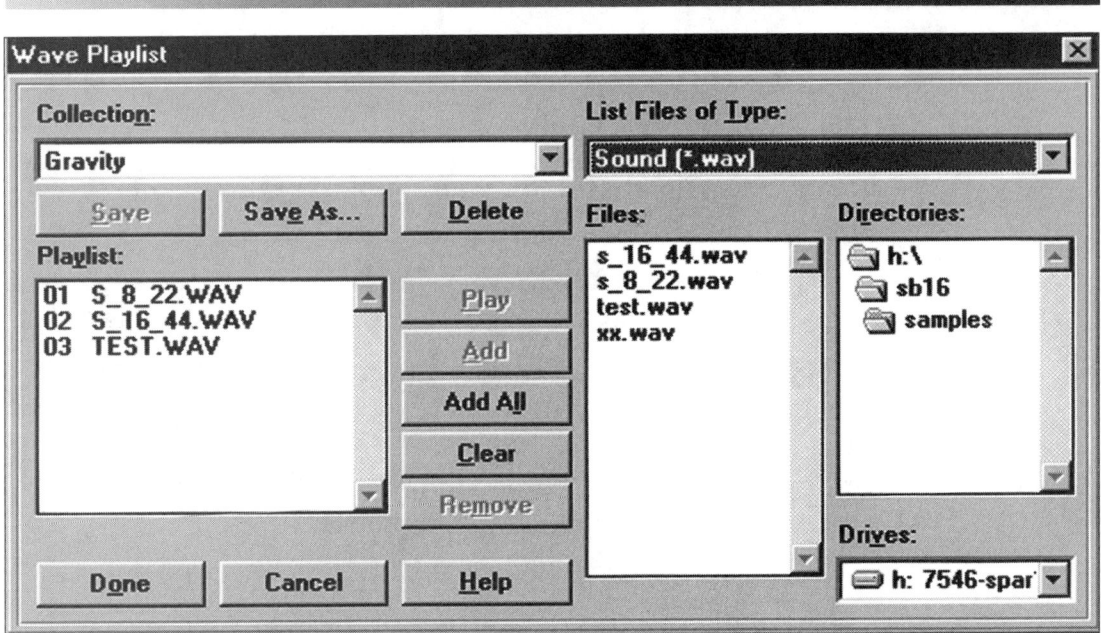

**Figure 2-21.**
The Wave Playlist
dialog

**3**   Click on the name of the wave file from the Files list that you want added to the Playlist. Click Done when you have the files you want. Clicking Cancel discards additions or changes to the Playlist.

## Adding Wave Files to a Playlist

**1**   Select the wave files as described before.

**2**   Click on Add to add chosen files to the Playlist. Clicking on Add All adds every wave file in the Files list to the playlist.

## Sampling Wave Files

It is easy to sample, or preview, wave files in a Playlist.

**1**   Select the files from the Playlist or Files list.

**2**   Click on Play to hear the file.

## Removing Files from a Playlist

**1**  Select the file from the Playlist.

**2**  Click on Remove to take it off the Playlist.

## Choosing Files on a Playlist

A quick way to choose several files for the Playlist is to use Ctrl or Shift (this works throughout your Windows applications, by the way).

- Press Ctrl while clicking with the mouse to choose files out of sequence.

- Press Shift and click on the first and last files in a list to choose a group of files in order.

## Reordering the Playlist Files

You can reorganize the sequence of your wave files by dragging files where you want them. Just click on the file name and hold down the right mouse button and drag it up or down the Playlist. Remember to use the right button—not the left like most other commands.

If you don't want to permanently change the order of your Playlist, use Shuffle to jumble things up a bit.

## Name the Playlist

You can keep your Playlists under different names for playback later. To name a Playlist, follow these steps:

**1**  Click on Save As from the Wave dialog.

**2**  Type the name of your new Playlist. In my example, I used the name, "Gravity."

**3**  Click on OK. If you click on Cancel, you won't save the named playlist but will return to the Playlist dialog.

# Keyboard Shortcuts for EnsembleWave

If you prefer using your keyboard instead of a mouse, you can control EnsembleWave with the commands in Table 2-3.

**Table 2-3.** Keyboard Commands for EnsembleWave

| Key | Action |
| --- | --- |
| A | Pause wave file |
| B | Play previous wave file |
| Ctrl - D | Change the "touch-sensitive" display |
| F | Play next wave file |
| F1 | Show on-line Help |
| G | Activate the Graphic Sound Control |
| H | Activate Shuffle (random playback) |
| I | Start Introduction mode (sample playback) |
| K | Rewind wave file |
| L | Open Playlist dialog box |
| M | Repeat mode |
| N | Minimize EnsembleWave to its icon |
| O | Exit EnsembleWave |
| P | Play current wave file |
| S | Stop playing wave file |
| Spacebar | Accept selection |
| T | Activate 2-digit mode |
| W | Fast-forward wave file |
| 0 -- 9 | Select wave file/sound file |

# EnsembleMIDI

What's a MIDI? It's an acronymn for "Musical Instrument Digital Interface," and it's a method to get instruments to communicate with each other and with a computer.

Why MIDI? It's a way to record and play back quality instrument sounds in a very efficient way. Small MIDI files contain directions for each note that's played—its pitch, duration and other information. The files can be "decoded" by your Sound Blaster's on-board synthesizer chip into instrument sounds. (From that point on, the synthesizer is just another audio source, like an audio CD.)

MIDI files have a ".MID" extension; for example, TEST.MID, and they're far smaller than digital audio (WAVE) files because they have only the "directions" for the sounds—not the actual sounds themselves. With the right applications, you can also change the key and tempo for a composition—something that would be very difficult with a digital audio file or CD.

If you want to connect external MIDI devices, such as keyboards, drum machines or synthesizers, to your Sound Blaster 16, you'll need an adapter and some cables. I've described those gadgets in Appendix A.

## Starting EnsembleMIDI

You can put EnsembleMIDI on your screen like the other EnsembleAV applications—either by double-clicking its icon in the Sound Blaster 16 program group, or by clicking the note button on EnsembleRemote. Here's what the EnsembleMIDI panel looks like:

Power Off button     "Touch Sensitive" Display     Playback Control

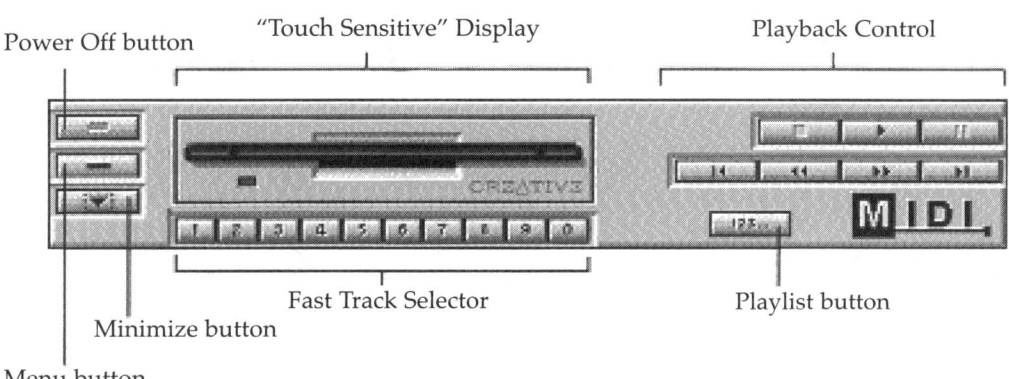

Fast Track Selector     Playlist button

Minimize button

Menu button

**Figure 2-22.**
EnsembleMIDI deck
explained

# Changing the "touch-sensitive" display

The "touch-sensitive" display has three different faces to choose from; it's almost identical to the display for EnsembleCD and EnsembleWave. Here's what you'll see in these displays:

**Figure 2-23.**
EnsembleMIDI
display panel

A "drive panel," that looks like a floppy drive. A little green light "comes on" when you're playing a MIDI file. You don't actually need to play MIDI files from a floppy drive; you can use the hard disk as well.

The currently selected MIDI file number ("track") and elapsed time for the file.

Title of the current MIDI file and playlist group.

For details of the display contents and buttons, refer to the EnsembleCD display in Figure 2-16; the MIDI transport is almost identical to the CD one.

## Using the Playlist

Because the EnsembleMIDI playlist is virtually the same as the EnsembleWave one, you can take a look back at Figure 2-21 and the discussion, to find out how to use it.

## Keyboard Shortcuts for EnsembleMIDI

If you'd rather use a keyboard instead of a mouse, you can control EnsembleMIDI with the commands in Table 2-4.

**Table 2-4.** Keyboard Commands for EnsembleMIDI

| Key | Action |
|---|---|
| A | Pauses MIDI file |
| Alt + Spacebar | Activates the menu |
| B | Play the previous track |
| Ctrl + D | Switch display mode |
| F | Play the next track |

| | |
|---|---|
| F1 | Access on-line help |
| G | Select the Graphic Slider |
| H | Toggle Shuffle Mode |
| I | Toggle Introduction Mode |
| K | Fast-rewind the track |
| L | Launch the Playlist dialog |
| M | Toggle Repeat Mode |
| N | Minimize the deck |
| O | Shut off the player |
| P | Play a selected track |
| S | Stop playing the track |
| V | Graphic Volume Control |
| W | Fast-forward the track |
| 0 -- 9 | Select MIDI file |

Now you've seen all the applications that make up EnsembleAV. Impressed? You should be: these are powerful, easy and fun to use controls.

But there's more to come! Read on to discover other powerful Windows-based audio tools for your Sound Blaster 16.

# 3

# Sound Mixing: Volume, Tone and Balance Control

reative Mixer is a slick little Windows application that lets you control the volume for each of the Sound Blaster 16 audio sources for both record and playback. Each stereo source has a balance control, and there are master volume and tone controls.

It's called a "mixer" because it also blends dough for great-tasting pies and bread. (No, scratch that thought.) It's because all the input audio signals are blended together at the output. For example, you could be recording your voice picked up by a microphone, combined with a MIDI instrument track. Or, you could play an audio CD at the same time you're playing a WAVE file and singing along. Call it karaoke with a vengeance!

Creative Mixer looks like a panel of linear slider controls that would be at home in any fancy stereo, and you slide the graphical "knobs" using your mouse.

*Before you begin using Sound Blaster audio, be sure your inputs are the proper type and at the right level. An incorrect input could easily blow out Sound Blaster's input circuits. To set the initial values, see the section on Source Setup.*

*Also be sure your speakers are able to handle the volume levels you plan to use; small speakers are very easy to blow out.*

*I suggest you start with all volume controls at their minimum settings, and slowly increase them until you have the sounds at your chosen listening level. If you hear loud hum or severe distortion at moderate volume settings, check again that the inputs are properly connected, and at the right signal level.*

## Starting Creative Mixer

Launch Creative Mixer on your Windows screen by double-clicking on its icon, as displayed in the Sound Blaster 16 group window. Or, you can select it from the drop-down menu of any of the EnsembleAV applications, which I described in Chapter 2. The following application window pops up:

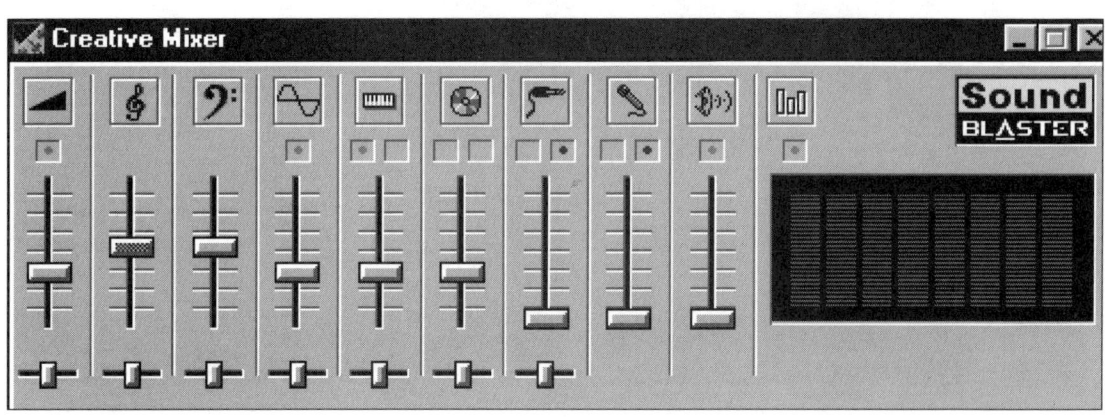

**Figure 3-1.**
Creative Mixer in all
its glory

This is the "expanded view;" you see not only the controls but also a graphic volume display at the right. Much more on that a little later. (If you're using Windows 95 and you have audio devices installed, your mixer may already be installed. Look for a little speaker at the right of the Toolbar. Click on that, and a volume slider appears; double-click and the complete mixer appears.)

## Audio Sources

Here's a quick list of the audio sources that Sound Blaster provides; I described them in Chapter 1 in serious detail:

**INPUTS**

| | |
|---|---|
| external LINE IN | low-level preamplifier audio |
| external MIC IN | dynamic microphone (mono) |
| internal CD AUDIO | from PC-mounted CD-ROM drive |
| internal digital audio | from WAVE files to D-to-A converter |
| internal MIDI | from FM synthesizer |

**OUTPUTS**

| | |
|---|---|
| LINE OUT | low-level preamplifier audio |
| SPK OUT | speaker audio (4W/channel max.) |
| PC speaker | speaker audio for PC speaker (mono) |
| internal digital audio | from D-to-A converter to WAVE files |

*On some Sound Blaster models, you choose between LINE OUT and SPK OUT using jumpers; see Appendix A.*

Here's a view of Creative Mixer's various parts, including the volume, balance and tone controls, and the "enable" buttons:

This is the "regular" view, missing the graphic display

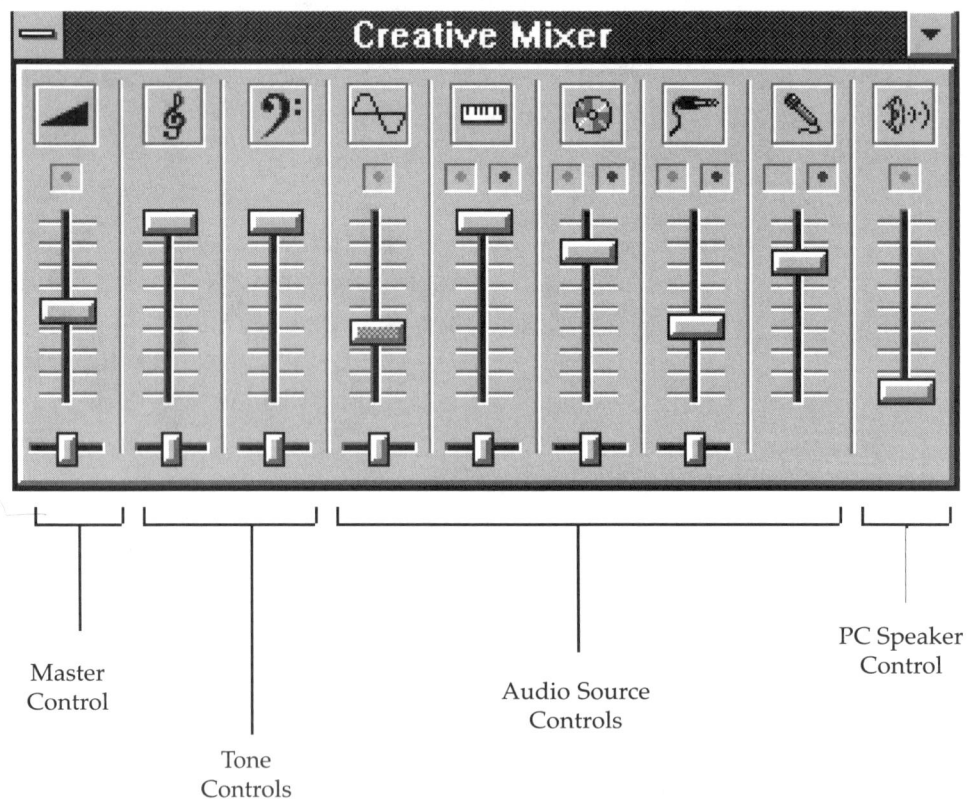

Master Control

Tone Controls

Audio Source Controls

PC Speaker Control

**Figure 3-2.**
Creative Mixer's sections

you saw in Figure 3-1 on page 45. (But soon, I'll return to visit that display soon.) Let's take a quick tour of the various sections, from left to right.

# Master Controls

| | | |
|---|---|---|
| Master Volume | wedge icon | controls the volume level of all audio sources |
| Treble | treble clef | adjusts higher tones of all audio sources |
| Bass | bass clef | adjusts lower tones of all audio sources |

# Source Audio Controls

| | | |
|---|---|---|
| WAVE | wave icon | digital audio from WAVE files |
| MIDI | keyboard icon | from Sound Blaster synthesizer |
| CD-audio | disk icon | from audio CD in CD-ROM |
| LINE IN | plug icon | external LINE IN audio |
| MIC | mic icon | external microphone in (mono) |
| PC Spkr | speaker icon | internal PC speaker (mono) |

# Balance Controls

Under each of the vertical "fader" slider controls is a smaller button. Slide it left and right to adjust balance for that sound source. Usually, you'll want the balance control to be in "dead-center," to send an equal amount of sound to both stereo speakers.

Of course, the microphone input and the PC speaker output don't have balance controls, because they're single-channel (monophonic).

# Source Enable Controls

Between the icons for each device and its volume control are sets of boxes, some with little dots in their center. These are graphic "switches" to turn each source on or off. Most audio sources have two boxes; the left one allows the source to play (go to the audio output), and the right one is for recording. Figure 3-3 on page 48 shows a close-up view of this section of Creative Mixer:

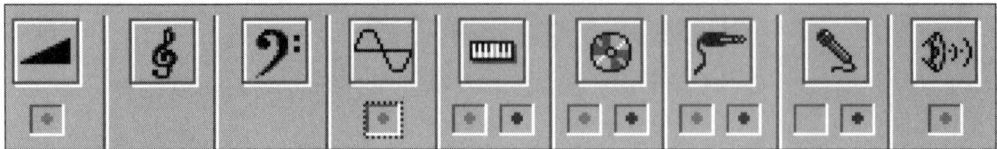

**Figure 3-3.**
Creative Mixer's
source enable
controls

In real life, the left dot is green and the right one is red. (The green one looks a bit fainter in these black-and-white illustrations.)

Click your mouse on a box to make the dot appear or disappear; this turns the source on or off. For example, in Figure 3-3, all the sources are enabled for both output *and* record *except for* the microphone. That's because microphone audio that gets to the speakers will usually produce feedback (a very unwelcome squeal).

*Feedback is caused when a signal keeps going around and around through an amplifier, building up steam each time until it's literally out of control. And really—who wants to be out of control? (A whole generation of electric guitar players who discovered how to use feedback effects as part of their music, that's who!)*

Three audio devices have single boxes (with green dots) only: the master volume at left, the digital audio (WAVE) source and the PC speaker volume at right. Two of these are *mute* buttons: click the one above master volume to turn all audio output on or off. Click the one for the PC speaker to turn PC sounds on or off. (The PC speaker gets its audio from a totally separate circuit—not from the Sound Blaster audio sources listed.)

The reason the WAVE source has only a green button is that it's the *only recorder* device that Sound Blaster controls. You can't record the recorder's recording!

# Control Menu

Want Creative Mixer to be setup your way? The Control Menu gives you lots of choices. Open this drop-down Windows menu list by clicking once on the top left button in the Title Bar (that strip at the top of the Mixer window). Title Bar not showing? Use your *right* mouse button to click most anywhere in the Mixer's window, to make the menu appear.

This control menu gives you the usual Windows controls to restore, move, minimize or close the Mixer application. But it also lets you choose:

- One of the three "views" of the Mixer, including a "Custom" view

- The contents of the custom view

- To turn the title bar on or off

- To turn the graphic display on or off

- Which audio sources to record, their level and channels

- The volume range (gain) for the audio output

- Windows help files for Creative Mixer

Let's take a closer look at these choices.

## Mixer Views

Creative mixer gives you three different screen appearances: the *minimum, expanded* and *custom* views. Turn to figure 3-4 on page 50 to see what they look like:

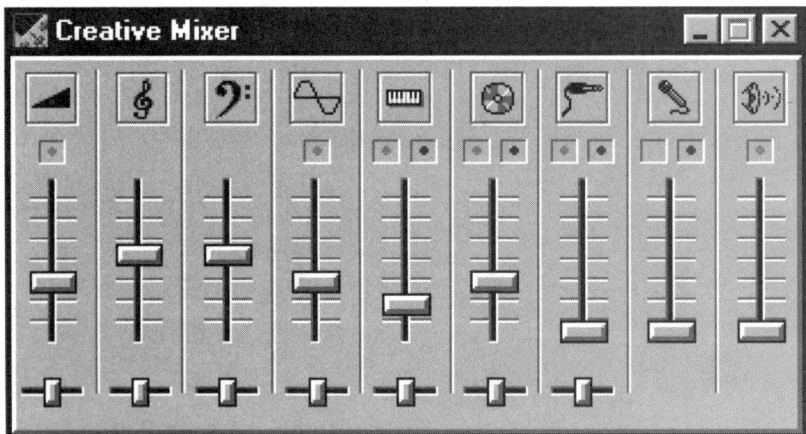

**Figure 3-4.**
Creative Mixer's
multiple views

The top figure is the *minimum* view; all it shows is the master volume slider. Once you've preset the other audio source controls, this may be all you'll need on your display. It's handy because it takes up so little space.

The second figure is the *expanded* view; it has the whole shebang—all possible slider controls. And finally, the *custom* view is a roll-your-own display: you decide what gets included. Here's how; click on Menu/Preferences and you'll get this box:

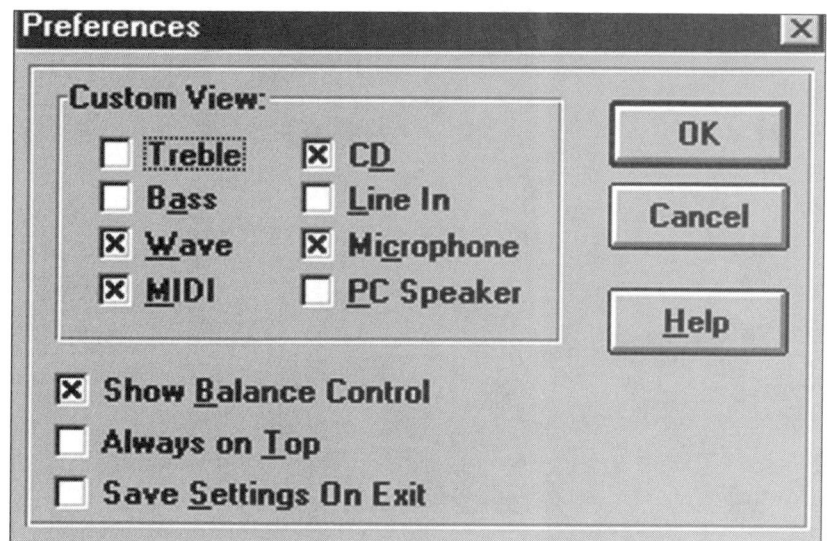

**Figure 3-5.**
Creative Mixer's
Preferences dialog

Just use your mouse to click the checkboxes for the sound sources you want displayed on custom view. And, if you click Creative Mixer to be "always on top," every time you click on a Windows application under it, the Mixer will stay in view. You can let your custom settings be temporary, or to make them permanent, click the "Save Settings on Exit" box.

The dialog box shown in this figure produced the custom view shown in Figure 3-4. I omitted the Treble, Bass, Line In and PC Speaker controls. (Note there's no checkbox for the Master Volume control; this control always appears in every view.)

## Title Bar

If you want the Windows-style title bar at the top of Creative Mixer, check that item on the drop-down menu. Or, double-click your mouse in any blank area on the Mixer display to turn the bar on or off. You may like the view without the bar, because it takes up less screen space.

## LED Display

You can add your choice of three "LED displays" to any of the Creative Mixer screen views shown in Figure 3-4 on page 50. These are vertical bar indicators that dynamically change with the audio output—much like the ones on stereo components.

Turn on the LED display by clicking its line on the drop-down menu. It appears connected to the right of your Mixer display, and looks like one of these:

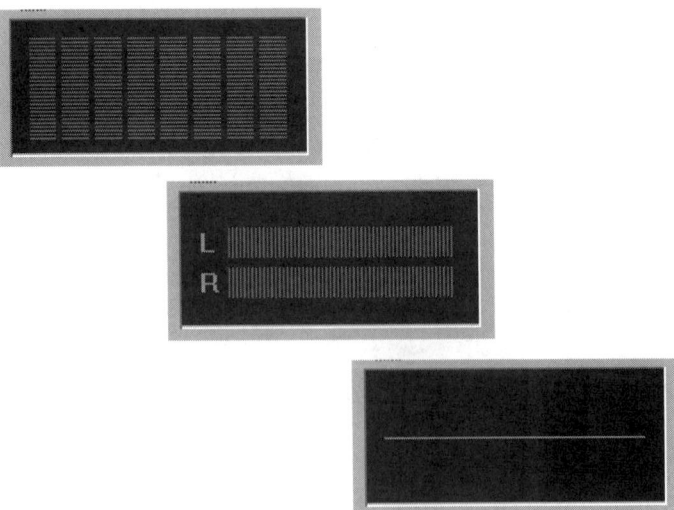

**Figure 3-6.**
Creative Mixer's "LED display"

The top display is a "graphic equalizer" that Creative Labs calls "Power Spectrum." It shows the audio level of both channels together, split into several frequency bands, from bass on the left to treble on the right. The middle display shows left and right audio levels—called a VU ("volume unit") meter. And the bottom one shows the waveform of the audio output—a "scope" display.

Once the LED display panel is in view, you can cycle through each of these three displays by clicking the mouse anywhere in the display box. You can turn audio to the display on or off by a click in the control box at the top left of the LED display section. A green dot shows that the display is turned on.

Whatever audio sources you're monitoring, the display must have *both* their red "record" and green output dots turned on and their individual gain slider turned up. The master volume and tone controls have no effect on the LED displa, and neither does the master balance control; but the source's individual balance control does.

(Unfortunately, the LED display isn't available when you're using the digital audio (WAVE) component; it simply blanks out. I'd like to monitor these displays most when I'm recording a WAVE file. The reason is that the same circuits on Sound Blaster that handle WAVE files are the ones that drive the LED display.)

## Recording Source Controls

Before you use the available sources for recording, you'll want to set up their inputs. Simply click on the Recording Settings line in the drop-down menu. You'll see this dialog box:

**Figure 3-7.**
Creative Mixer's
Recording settings
dialog

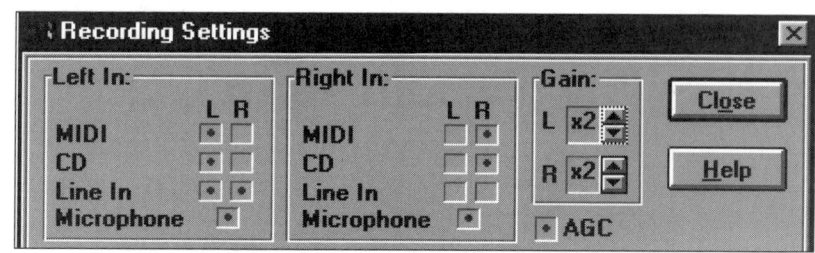

This is in effect, a "patch panel": you "plug" either left or right audio source to either left or right audio input. Figure 3-7 on page 53 shows, most of the sources are connected in the usual way, left source to left input and right source to right input. But, because I knew my (external) Line In signal was to be single channel (monophonic), I enabled the left Line In to both left and right channels.

Of course, if you forget to click on either channel, you won't be able to record any audio from that source. And don't forget to enable each source by clicking its red "record" box in the main Mixer display as well.

If your overall recording gain (level) is a bit too high or low, you can adjust it here, separately for each channel. (Ordinarily, you'll use the same setting for both channels.) If the signal is weak, and you have to set your gain sliders near the top of the range to get a good recording level, increase the gain. If the signal is distorted or overloaded, even if the gain slider is turned low, decrease the overall gain . In figure 3-7, I'm using "2X" gain. Your choices are between 1X, 2X and 4X.

Finally, I've clicked the "AGC" box; this stands for "Automatic Gain Control," and affects only the microphone input. When it's turned on, it adjusts the mic volume automatically to try to keep recording levels within a useful range. You'll want to use AGC for voice recordings, because people's speech varies so much in volume. But for music, with its dynamic sound ranges, AGC may make the recording effect too "flat." Experiment!

## Output Gain Control

Finally, you have an adjustment for output levels for each channel. When you click the Menu line for Output Gain, you get the following little box:

**Figure 3-8.**
Creative Mixer's
Output gain dialog
box

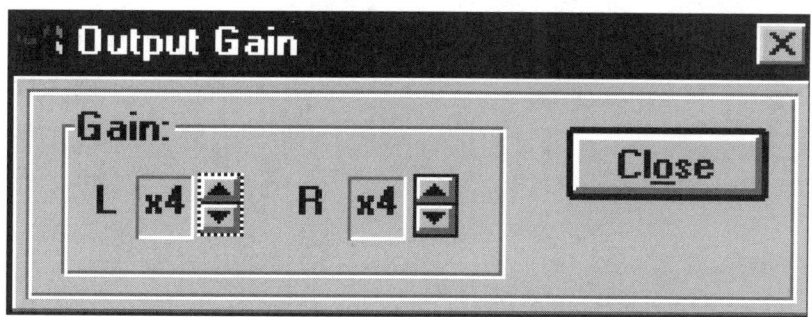

Your choices are 1X, 2X or 4X. Here, I've set Sound Blaster outputs with a 4X (highest-level) sound output. You'll know you've set the gain too high if you get distortion at moderate levels from all sources. It's too low if you turn the gain way up and still don't have enough level. (But don't blame low speaker volume on gain level alone; your speakers may need more power than the little on-board power amplifier can provide. If so, your answer is to use an external amplifier or powered speakers. Take a look at Chapter 1 for more information.

## Help for Creative Mixer

Check the Help line on the drop-down Menu, and you'll get graphic and useful information about Creative Mixer. Or, you can simply press the "F1" function key for the same help.

## Leaving Creative Mixer

Is it time to leave Creative Mixer? You have three ways to do it:

- Open the Control Menu and click on Close.

- Double-click on the Control Menu box in the upper left corner of the window.

- Press [Alt] and [F4] together.

## Keyboard Shortcuts for Creative Mixer

If you prefer, you can use keyboard entries instead of mouse clicks to control this application. When you do this, Creative Mixer must be the application in *focus* (the one that's selected on your Windows desktop).

Here are the keyboard entries that control Creative Mixer:

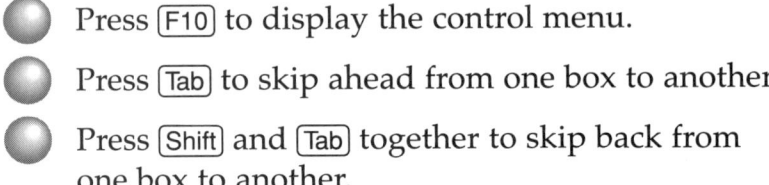

- Press F10 to display the control menu.
- Press Tab to skip ahead from one box to another.
- Press Shift and Tab together to skip back from one box to another.
- Press ↑ or ↓ to adjust volume, tone, or gain.
- Press Esc to hide or display the Title Bar.

Creative Mixer is a handy tool, always ready to help you control audio levels and record and playback features. But it's time to read on to the next chapter, to the most elaborate audio tool in your Sound Blaster bag of tricks: CreativeWaveStudio. You're going to be impressed!

# Creative WaveStudio

Y ou've recorded a perfectly good digital audio (WAVE) file using CreativeWave and now you want to mess it up. Good! Creative WaveStudio is your tool. With it (and the help this chapter gives you), you can edit, cut, and paste audio segments of any WAVE recording to move them anywhere you like. You can add special effects and do over-dubbing and other spectacular audio gymnastics. You can even open and work with multiple WAVE files at once!

CreativeWaveStudio is a graphic sound editor. That means it shows you audio as *waveforms*: visual "pictures" of sound. To best understand this tool, you need just a little background in audio terms and concepts.

## Making Waves About Sound

Sound is that stuff that fills our ears all day (that, and earwax, of course). But how can we select sound and edit it? Picture any sound as a set of waves; just as a rock dropped in a pond makes ripples on its surface, a sound pushes out waves of air from its source.

Now, if we could only take a picture of those waves, we could better understand, control, and shape the sound. With Creative WaveStudio, we can.

The term for the speed the waves ripple (which makes them closer or farther apart from each other) is *frequency*. Sounds that have higher frequency have higher musical pitch; a piccolo has a higher pitch than a tuba. Frequency is measured by counting the number of waves—or cycles—the sound waves make each second; the measuring unit for this is hertz, abbreviated Hz.

The height or strength of the waves is its *amplitude*. A higher wave makes a louder sound. Too high, and the wave will sink your boat (I mean, blow out your eardrums).

Creative WaveStudio (I'll just call it WaveStudio) puts a graph on your video display that shows the frequency and amplitude of the sounds you record. This graph is called—you guessed it: a *waveform.*

The higher the waveform, the louder the sound; the closer the waves are packed together, the higher the frequency (that is, the musical pitch).

Because music and voices usually contain bunches of waves with different frequencies and amplitudes all mixed together, the waveform you see is usually pretty jumbled looking. If you want a simple one to look at, try whistling a single tone into your microphone. A simple clear tone like this is called a *sine wave,* but it rarely occurs in music (perhaps from a piccolo).

# WaveStudio Editing Concepts

Because WaveStudio is very graphic, it's really easy to use.

First, remember that you'll be working with digital audio files in the industry-standard WAVE format. Tiny pieces of sound are stored as *samples;* the more samples that are stored each second, the better fidelity the stored audio. The size of the sample (8 or 16 bits) is another factor; the larger the sample, the better the stored audio. More on this later.

To edit a WAVE file, you open it with WaveStudio. It appears as a waveform you can see in a Preview window. From the entire waveform, you select a segment to edit, which appears in an Edit window. In the Edit window, you can very accurately isolate the sound portion you want to work with.

You can cut and paste these audio segments, add special effects such as echo, pan, reverse and invert, over-dub and otherwise mangle the original sounds. Combine portions of several open WAVE files if you like; when you're done, store the result as a new WAVE file.

# Starting WaveStudio and the main display

Launch WaveStudio by double-clicking on its icon in the Sound Blaster 16 group window. Here's what you'll see:

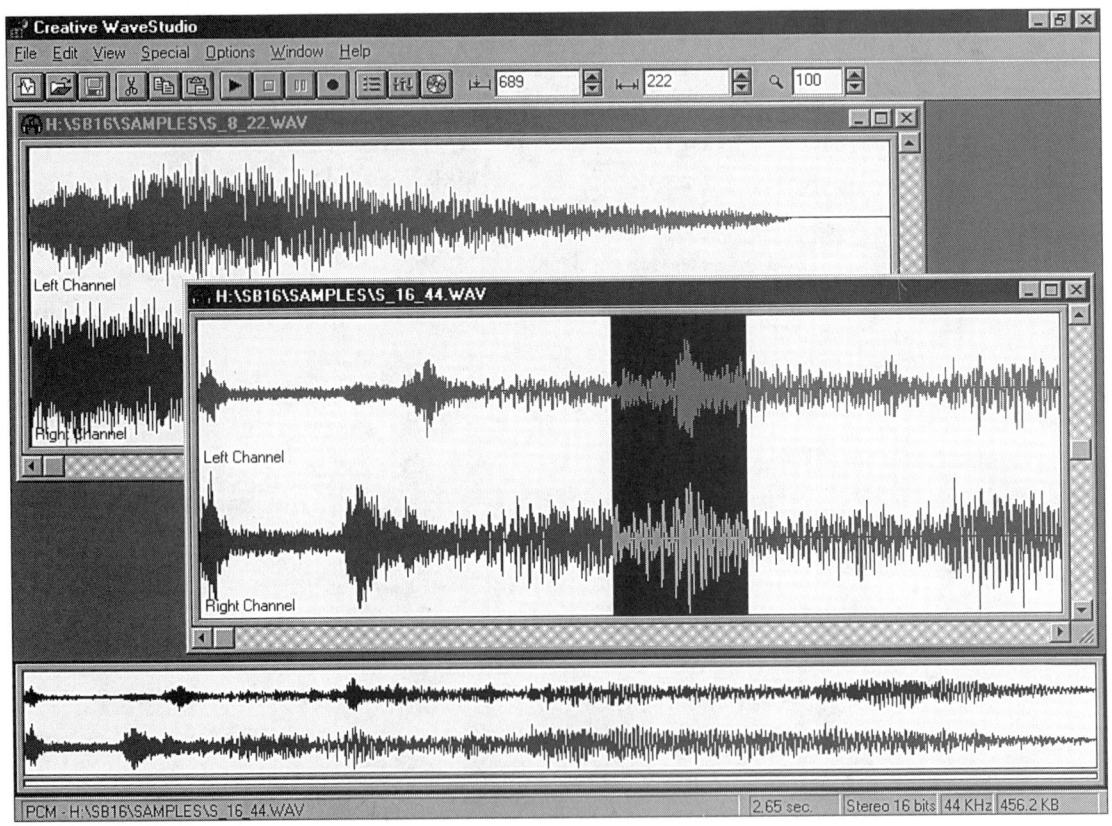

**Figure 4-1.**
Creative WaveStudio's screen

A lot is going on in this display, so hang in there while I "take it apart" for you. These are the main sections:

- Toolbar and menus at top
- Audio edit window or windows in the middle
- Preview window at bottom
- Status bar at bottom edge

*You'll need a mouse to use WaveStudio. Although you can use the keyboard to access commands from the Menu Bar, the mouse click-and-drag is your only means to reach the toolbar and to select wave segments.*

*If you click on the right mouse button, a special short menu of often-used functions pops up. Give it a try!*

## Toolbar

For fast access, most of the frequently-used WaveStudio commands are available as icons on a Toolbar at the top of the screen, just a mouse-click away. Just above the Toolbar is the Menu, with dozens of features you can access with the mouse or from the keyboard. Because the Menu is so intense, I'll give you its details after a quick review of the rest of the display. Here's how the Toolbar looks:

**Figure 4-2.**
WaveStudio Toolbar
(with Menu)

**Table 4-1.** WaveStudio Toolbar Buttons and Boxes

| Name | Function |
|------|----------|
| New | Create a new, empty window |
| Open | Select an existing WAVE (.WAV) file for edit |
| Save | Record the active wave file to disk |
| Cut | Move the selected section of the active WAVE file to the Windows clipboard |
| Copy | Copy the selected section of the active WAVE file to the clipboard |
| Paste | Insert the selected WAVE file segment on the clipboard into the selected edit window |

CONTINUED ON PAGE 62

CONTINUED FROM
PAGE 61

| | |
|---|---|
| Play | Play the selected segment of the active WAVE file |
| Stop | Stop playing the WAVE file segment |
| Pause | Pause/resume playing the WAVE file segment |
| Record | Record a new WAVE file |
| Format | Open the Record Settings dialog box |
| Mixer | Launch Creative Mixer (to set volume levels) |
| Position | Set the starting position of the WAVE selection (enter a number or use the arrow scroll buttons) |
| Size | Set the length of the wave selection (enter a number or use the arrow scroll buttons) |
| Zoom | Set the zoom factor of the file shown (enter a number or use the arrow scroll buttons) |

## Edit Windows

When you open a WAVE file for editing, its waveform appears in an Edit window. You can have several files open at once—each in its own window. You can set the position and size of the active sample in each window by clicking and dragging your mouse. (This section is reverse-highlighted in the figure.) This has the same effect as entering the Position and Size in the boxes at top right on the toolbar.

You can set the zoom factor for the active window by using your mouse to move the "elevator" up and down the scroll bar at right. The visual effect is to "spread out" or "squeeze up" the waveform in the active window. (This is the same result as setting the zoom factor in the far-right toolbar box.)

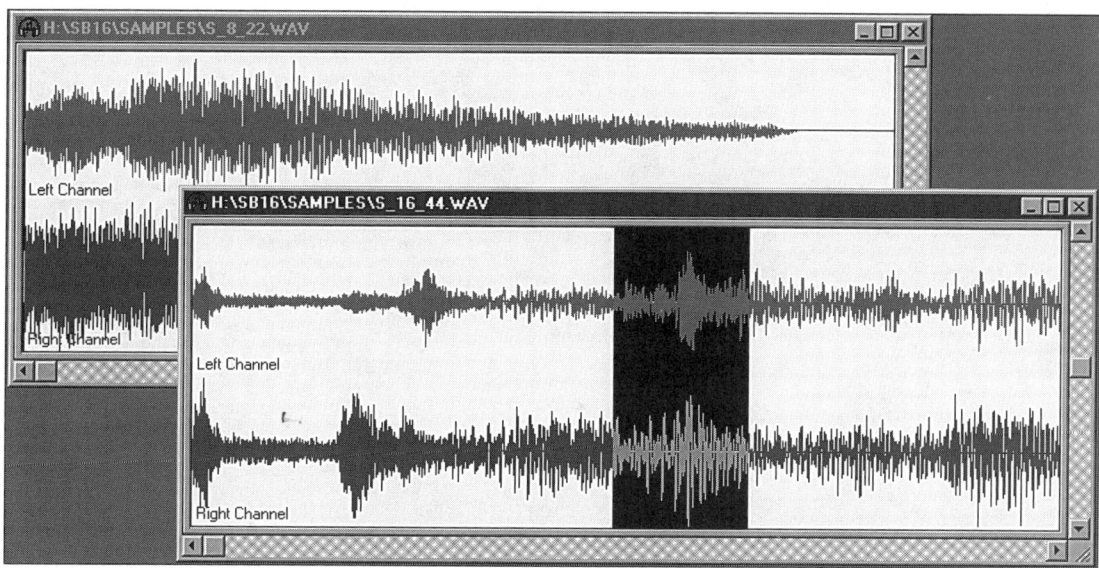

**Figure 4-3.**
WaveStudio's Edit windows (with two files open)

# Preview Window

This window (at the bottom of the screen) shows the waveform for the entire WAVE file that's in the active Edit window at top. Here, you get the "big picture" so you can quickly locate the audio segments you want to edit.

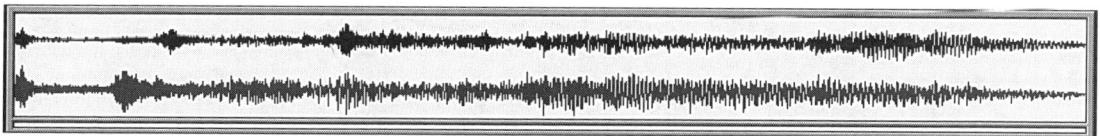

**Figure 4-4.**
WaveStudio's Preview window

Simply click and drag your mouse to select a segment, and it's also selected and highlighted in the Edit window above.

Built into the bottom edge of the Preview window is a thin stripe: the Progress bar. When you click on the Play icon on the Toolbar, the portion of this bar under your sample changes color and expands to underline what's being played.

## Status Bar

At the bottom of the window is a thin bar that shows the status of the active file. Here it is:

| PCM - H:\SB16\SAMPLES\S_16_44.WAV | 2.65 se |

On the left are the drive, directory, and file name. At right are the duration of the file, and its format (Stereo / 16 bit sample / 44 kHz sample rate) and size (456.2 Kb).

## Menu Features

Back to the Menus, that first appeared in Figure 4-2 on page 63, just above the Toolbar. Here they are again:

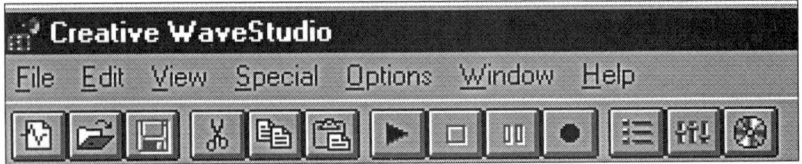

(Now that you've seen the quick tour, this menu should make more sense.)

Eight menu groups are on the Menu bar. They are:

| | | |
|---|---|---|
| ● | File | new / open / close / save commands |
| ● | Edit | File cut / copy / paste / delete / crop / select commands |
| ● | View | Screen display features / edit view features |
| ● | Special | Audio special effects |
| ● | Options | Display settings / Record settings / Mixer launch |
| ● | Window | Window arrangements |
| ● | Help | Windows graphical help |

To select a file item, click on the key word on the file menu and a drop-down list of choices appears. Click on an item on this list to select the action you want.

Or, you can enter the key letter of your choice on the keyboard (the key letter is the one underlined in the key word). Hold the [Alt] key down, and type the key letter. For example, to save a file, type [Alt]+[F], then [S].

Now for the details:

## File Menu

**Table 4-2** File Menu Commands

| Command | Action |
| --- | --- |
| New | Opens a new, empty Edit window |
| Open | Opens an existing WAVE file |
| Close | Closes the active Edit window |
| Close All | Closes all open Edit window. |
| Save | Saves the active Edit window under its original name |
| Save As | Saves the active Edit window with a new name |
| Save All | Saves all open Edit windows |
| Exit | Quits WaveStudio |
| 1--4 | The last four open files are listed at the bottom of the File list; to open one, click on the file name |

## Edit Menu

**Table 4-3.** Edit Menu Commands

| Command | Action |
|---|---|
| Undo | Returns the active file to the last saved version |
| Cut | Moves selected section of wave file to the clipboard |
| Copy | Copies selected section of wave file to the clipboard |
| Paste | Inserts most recent cut or copied section of WAVE file. You can highlight a section to replace with inserted data. If you don't select anything, Paste inserts the data at the cursor position. |
| Paste Mix... | Mixes cut or copied section of a WAVE file with the active file. This allows you to play two wave files together. |
| Delete | Removes copied section of a wave file |
| Crop to Selection | Deletes entire file except section you highlight |
| Select All | Highlights entire wave file. Double-clicking the mouse in the Edit window does this, also. |

# View Menu

**Table 4-4.** View Menu Commands

| Command | Action |
|---------|--------|
| <u>P</u>review | Turns on the Preview window at the bottom of the screen. Click on Preview again (removing the check mark) to turn the window off. |
| <u>T</u>oolbar | Turns on the toolbar at the top of the screen. Click on Toolbar again (removing the check mark) to turn the bar off. |
| <u>S</u>tatus Bar | Turns on the status bar at the bottom of the screen. Click on Status Bar again (removing the check mark) to turn the bar off. |
| <u>F</u>it Wave to Window | Zooms in or out, to fit the entire waveform in the Edit window. |
| <u>A</u>ctual Size | Sets the wave display to its "normal" size (zoom ratio of 1:1). |
| <u>C</u>ursor Position | Displays waveform at beginning point of selection. |
| Cursor <u>E</u>nd | Displays waveform at ending point of selection. |
| <u>Z</u>oom | Expands the selected section to fill the Edit window |

# Special Menu

**Table 4-5.** Special Menu Commands

| Command | Action |
|---|---|
| Reverse | Plays entire or highlighted section of file in reverse (yes, backwards). You can reverse either or both stereo channels. (Can this feature help country-music lovers retrieve their lost dogs, trucks, homes and lovers?) |
| Add Echo | Adds an echo effect to an entire or high-lighted section of file. You can apply echo to either or both channels of stereo files. |
| Invert Waveform | Inverts wave for the entire highlighted section of a file. You can invert either or both channels of stereo files. |
| Rap! | Instant repeat: makes a copy of the selected section and puts it in the file next to the section. |
| Insert Silence | Inserts a silent segment to the left of selected section of file of the same length as the selected section |
| Force to Silence | Replaces selected section of file with silence. You can silence either or both channels of stereo files. |
| Fade In | Fades in to entire or selected section of file by slowly raising volume. You can fade in to either or both channels of stereo files. |

| | |
|---|---|
| Fade Out | Fades out of entire or selected section of file by slowly lowering volume. You can fade out of either or both channels of stereo files. |
| Swap Channels | For stereo files, trades entire or selected sections of file between the left and right channels. |
| Pan Left to Right | For stereo files, moves the entire or selected section of a file to the right channel, leaving the left channel empty. The cleared channel is free for your own input. |
| Pan Right to Left | For stereo files, moves the entire or selected section of a file to the left channel, leaving the right channel empty. The cleared channel is free for your own input. |
| Phase Shift | For stereo files, delays playback of one or both channels of the entire or selected file. |
| Convert Format | Converts the format of the selected file to another sample rate and sample size |
| Modify Frequency | Changes the playback rate of the entire file between three sample rates, changing the frequency by the same factor. |
| Amplify Volume | Changes the volume of the entire or selected section of a file for either or both channels. |

## Options Menu

**Table 4-6.** Options Menu Commands

| Command | Action |
| --- | --- |
| <u>R</u>ecord Settings | Selects stereo, mono, sampling rate and sampling size |
| <u>M</u>ixer Settings | Starts Creative Mixer |
| <u>C</u>ustomize Colors | Changes the way Wave Studio looks on your screen |
| Display in <u>B</u>ytes | Shows wave file information in bytes |
| Display in <u>S</u>amples | Shows wave file information in samples |
| Display in <u>M</u>illiseconds | Shows wave file information in milliseconds |
| <u>A</u>lways on Top | Floats WaveStudio on top of all open Windows applications |

## Window Menu

**Table 4-7.** Window Menu Commands

| Command | Action |
| --- | --- |
| <u>C</u>ascade | Shows all open windows stacked, off-set style, on top of each other |
| Tile <u>H</u>orizontally | Tile all open windows horizontally |
| <u>T</u>ile vertically | Tile all open windows vertically |
| <u>A</u>rrange Icons | Arrange the icons for all minimized windows at the bottom of the window |
| 1--5 | List of open files. To switch to an open file's window, click on the file name shown or press the number of the file you want |

# Help Menu

**Table 4-8.** Windows Help Menu Commands

| Command | Action |
|---|---|
| Contents | Shows a table of contents for WaveStudio help |
| Search for Help | Lets you ask for information on any topic; type the topic name in the supplied box |
| System Information | Shows system setup, available resources, free memory, and disk space |
| About WaveStudio | A cute scrollbox with names of the Creative Labs development team and a short audio clip |

# Mixing Wave Files

WaveStudio helps you format, open, save, and mix (combine) wave files.

## Format

You need to choose wave sample rate and size before converting formats or recording a new wave file. Specify the format by clicking on Options/Record Settings from the menu bar. This dialog sets the channel type, sampling rate, and sample size:

**Figure 4-7.**
Record Settings
dialog

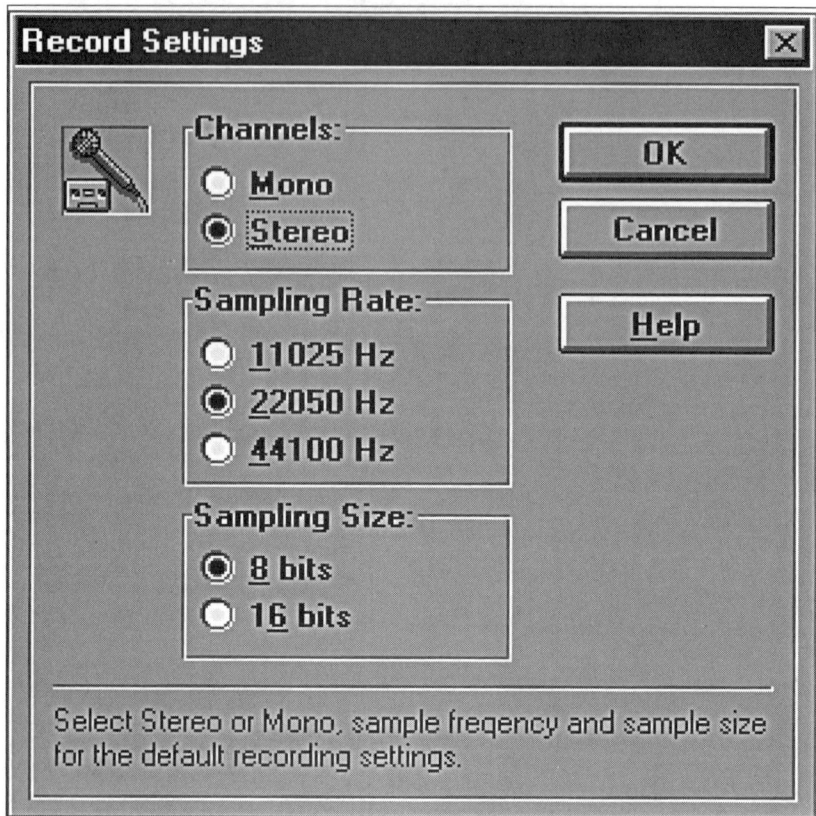

Choose the following from the dialog box:

**1**     Choose mono or stereo under Channels.

**2**     Select a sampling rate of 11026 Hz for voice recording, 22050 Hz for recording from a cassette tape, or 44100 Hz for recording from a CD.

**3**     Choose a sampling size of 8 bits or 16 bits. Eight bits gives you sound quality like a tape or the wave files that you got with Windows (the Chimes, Ding, and Tada .WAV files in your WINDOWS directory). Sixteen-bit audio is almost CD-quality.

*When it comes to digital audio, bigger is better — larger sampling and more bits make for a higher-fidelity, lower-noise wave file. But bigger is also* much *bigger. For example, ten seconds of a stereo, 16-bit, 44 kHz sample rate wave file gobbles up over 1.7* megabytes *of disk space. Yet a ten-second mono, 8-bit, 11 kHz recording needs only 110 kilobytes — one-sixteenth as much. You'll want to use the better-quality formats only when the audio source justifies them — and be ready with a monster hard disk.*

## Opening Wave Files

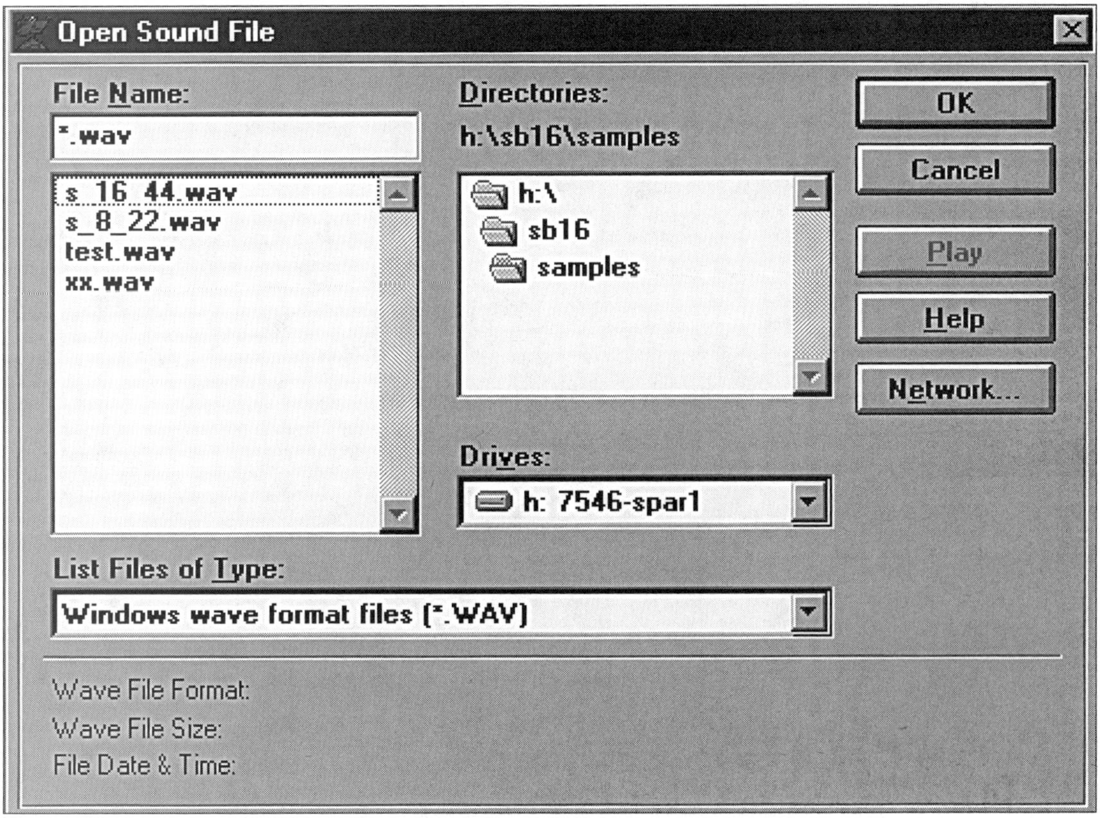

**Figure 4-8.**
Open Sound File
dialog

The menu command, File / Open lets you open an existing WAVE file. (You can also click on the open file folder icon on the Toolbar.) This gives you the Open Sound File dialog box:

**Open Sound File**

**File Name:**
`*.wav`

s_16_44.wav
s_8_22.wav
test.wav
xx.wav

**Directories:**
h:\sb16\samples

h:\
  sb16
    samples

**Drives:**
h: 7546-spar1

OK
Cancel
Play
Help
Network...

**List Files of Type:**
Windows wave format files (*.WAV)

Wave File Format:
Wave File Size:
File Date & Time:

Pick the file you want by clicking on its file name, then click on OK. You can also open a file by double-clicking on the file name.

You also may need to select the drive and directory that holds the file. Simply scroll through the Directories list or click the Drive listbox and make your choices.

*You can also open and edit some rarely-used formats. Files produced by the CreativeVoice application (more on this in another chapter) have an extension of .VOC. Certain data files called "raw" have an extension (can you believe it?) of .RAW. When you open these types of files, WaveStudio will later let you save them as wave (.WAV) format files.*

You may also be able to open a file using "drag-'n-drop;" highlight the file on the File Names list, hold down the right mouse button, drag the cursor to the Edit window area, and release the mouse button. To open several files at once, hold down the ⇧Shift key while clicking on the file names you want.

## Recording Wave Files

To record a wave file in WaveStudio, follow these steps:

**1**    Click on the the Toolbar's New icon (the blank page with a wave in it). This opens a new (empty) edit window.

**2**    Click on the Toolbar Record icon (the red dot). The New Recording dialog box pops up (See figure 4-9 on page 75).

**3**    Verify the Recording Level settings in the top two bars of the New Recording dialog box. Adjust if needed by clicking on the Mixer button; this pops up Creative Mixer.

**New Recording...**                                                            ☒

┌─ Recording Level: ──────────────────────────────────┐          ┌──────────┐
│                                                      │          │  Start   │
│  [                                              ]    │          └──────────┘
│  Left channel                                        │          ┌──────────┐
│                                                      │          │  Cancel  │
│  [                                     ] [ Mixer... ]│          └──────────┘
│  Right channel                                       │          ┌──────────┐
└──────────────────────────────────────────────────────┘         │ Settings...│
┌─ Record To File: ───────────────────────────────────┐          └──────────┘
│                                                      │          ┌──────────┐
│  h:\sb16\samples                                     │          │ CD Player│
│                                                      │          └──────────┘
│  [record.wav                       ] [ Browse... ]   │          ☐ CD Sync
│                                                      │          ┌──────────┐
└──────────────────────────────────────────────────────┘         │   Help   │
                                                                  └──────────┘

Recording Format:            Stereo 8 bits, 22050 Hz
Available Disk Space:        14188544 bytes
Recording Time (maximum):    321 seconds

**Figure 4-9.**
New Recording
dialog

**4**   Check the record format at the bottom of the dialog box; adjust if needed by clicking on the Settings button. This pops up the same dialog you saw in Figure 4-7 on page 72.

**5**   Enter or confirm the file name for your recording in the Record to File box. To look for an existing file, click on the Browse button.

**6**   Verify the Available Disk Space total shown at the bottom of the dialog box; if there isn't enough room for the new file, select another drive with more space. (Or, you can exit WaveStudio and delete some old files.)

**8**   Click on Start

*Note the CD-Sync checkbox. If you're using EnsembleCD as your audio source, and this box is checked, the CD will automatically start playing when you start your WAVE recording. Click on the CD Player button to pop up the EnsembleCD application.*

## Recording Over an Old File

Follow these steps to replace a file with a new recording:

**1**    Open an existing file

**2**    Click on the Record icon

**3**    Fill out this Record Over dialog when it appears:

```
Record Over - [H:\SB16\SAMPLES\S_8_22.WAV]                    [X]

 ┌─Recording Level:────────────────────────┐      ┌─────────┐
 │                                          │      │  Start  │
 │ [                                     ]  │      └─────────┘
 │ Left channel                             │      ┌─────────┐
 │                                          │      │ Cancel  │
 │ [                           ] ┌────────┐ │      └─────────┘
 │                               │ Mixer..│ │      ┌─────────┐
 │ Right channel                 └────────┘ │      │CD Player│
 └──────────────────────────────────────────┘      └─────────┘
                                                    □ CD Sync

                                                    ┌─────────┐
                                                    │  Help   │
                                                    └─────────┘

 Recording Format:         Stereo 8 bits, 22050 Hz
 Available Disk Space:      14188544 bytes
 Recording Time (maximum):  321 seconds
```

**Figure 4-10.**
Record Over dialog

## Saving Wave Files

You can save a wave file under its existing name (or name and save a new file) with the Save command. To save a wave file under a new name or change its type or format, use Save As.

## Using Save

**1** Choose Save from the File menu or click on the Save icon from the Toolbar. Here's the dialog box:

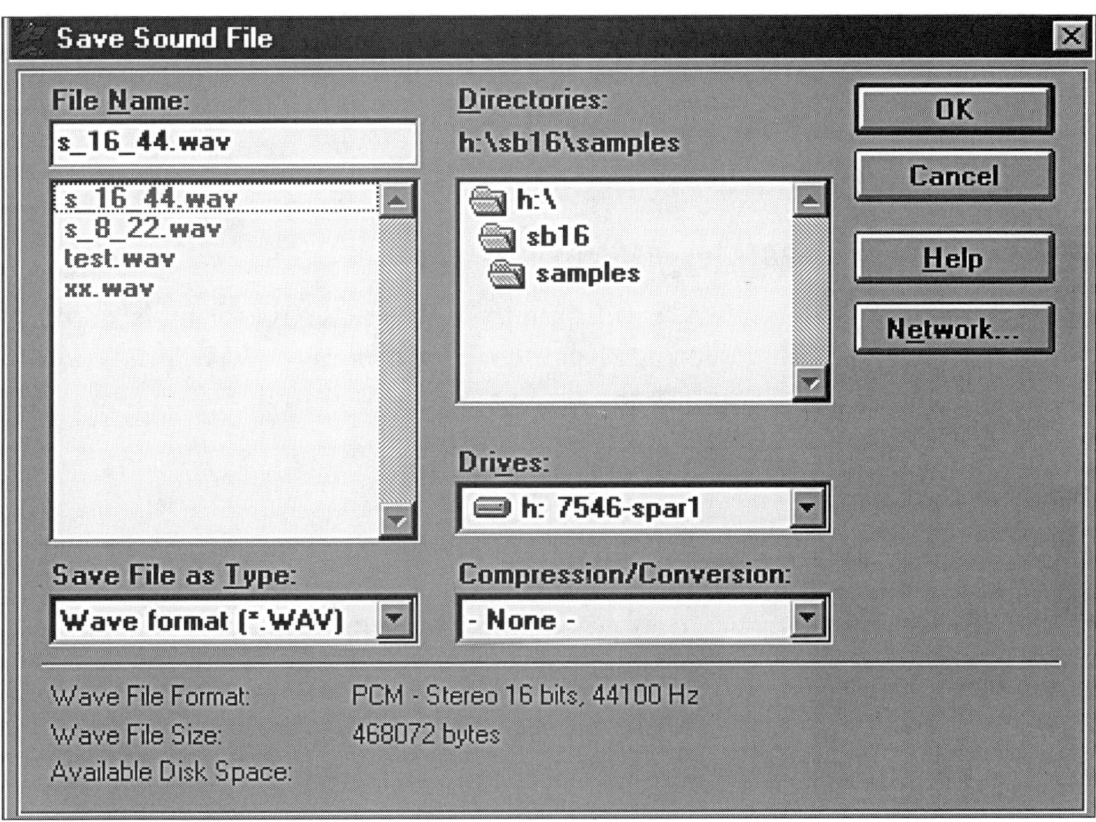

**Figure 4-11.**
Save Sound dialog

**2** Type the name and path (drive and directory) if needed

**3** Click on OK

## Using Save As

**1** Choose Save As from the File menu; the Save As dialog appears as in Figure 4-11 above.

2    Type the name and path (drive and directory)
      if needed.

3    Change the file type or
      Compression/Conversion format. Choose from
      the Compression/Conversion list to convert a
      file.You have a choice of a half-dozen formats
      for 16-bit files, but only PCM for 8-bit files.

4    Click on OK

## Mixing Wave Files

You can "mix" data from two wave files; that is, combine
their sounds together. To mix two wave files, follow
these steps:

1    Open both wave file

2    In the edit window for one file, highlight and
      select the part of the waveform you want, or
      double-click in the Edit window to select the
      whole file.

3    Click on Copy or Cut from the Edit menu (or
      the icons on the Toolbar) to place the data in a
      buffer. (Copy doesn't change the waveform, but
      Cut deletes the selected segment from the
      waveform as it saves it aside.

4    Select the second file's Edit window

5    Place the cursor in the starting position where
      you want to mix the copied waveform on top of
      this one. If you want to replace a section of this
      waveform instead, drag the mouse to highlight
      the section.

6    Click on Paste Mix from the Edit menu; the
     Paste Mix box appears:

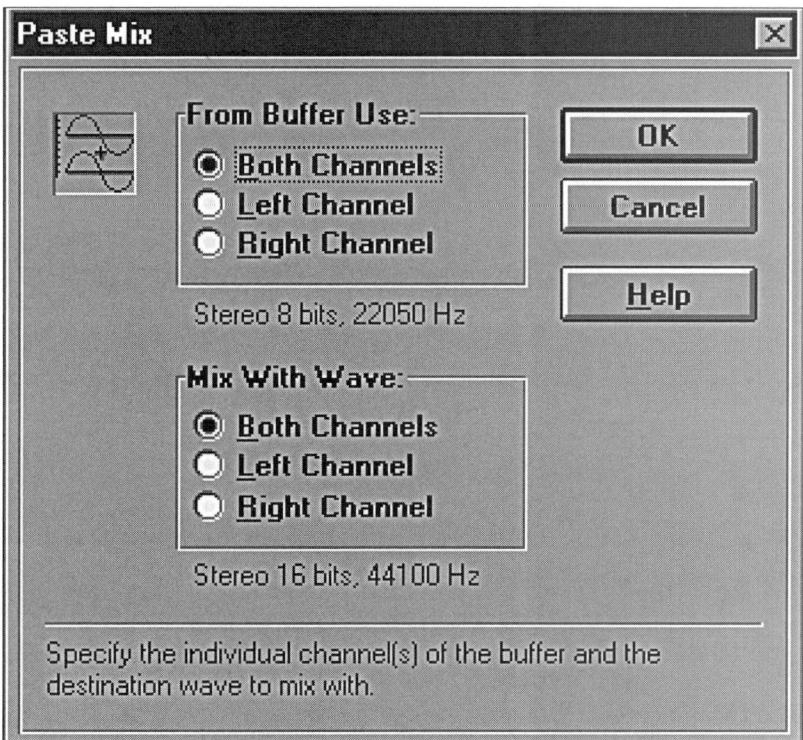

**Figure 4-12.**
Paste Mix dialog

7    Here, you can choose which channels to use
     from the copied data in the buffer and the tar-
     get file in the Edit window. You can only mix
     files that have the same sampling size (8- or 16-bit); if
     they are different, use Convert Format from the
     Special menu to change the sampling of one file.

## Adding Special Effects

If you're a true sound cruncher, here comes your bag of
tricks for very nasty effects. Before you indulge, why not
make a backup copy of that favorite WAVE file? Then
you can experiment as much as you like, and be able to

start fresh if you choose. Here's the list of effects on the Special menu:

- Reverse
- Add Echo
- Invert Waveform
- Rap!
- Insert Silence
- Force to Silence
- Fade In/Out
- Swap Channels
- Pan Left to Right/Right to Left
- Phase Shift
- Convert Format
- Modify Frequency
- Amplify Volume

## Reverse a File

Shades of *Abby Road*! (Oops, I'm showing my age.) With this option you can play an entire file or highlighted section of it in reverse (backward). Here's how:

**1**    Click on Reverse from the Special menu; this dialog appears:

**2**    Choose the channels to play in reverse, then click on OK

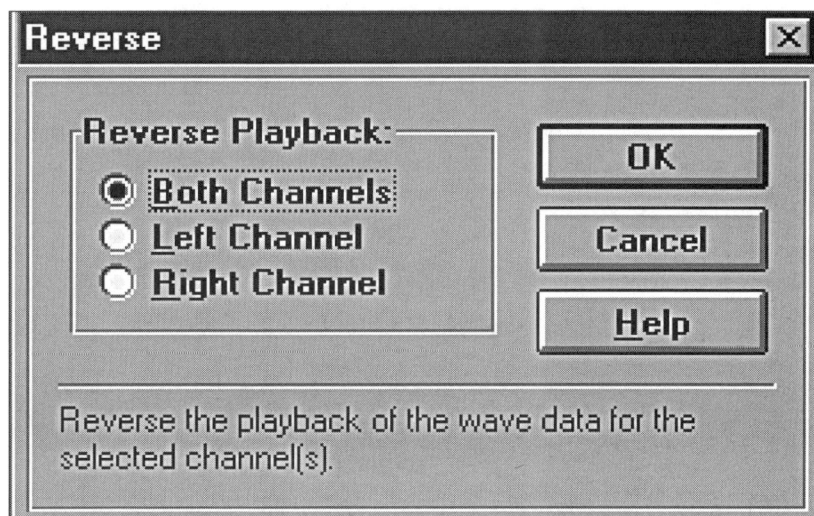

**Figure 4-13.**
Reverse dialog

## Add Echo to a File

This adds an echo to the wave file, like shouting into a
canyon (or a metal wastebasket). To add an echo:

**1**   Click on Add Echo from the special menu, and
what appears but:

**2**   Use Magnitude to select the percentage of the
sound that contributes to the echo

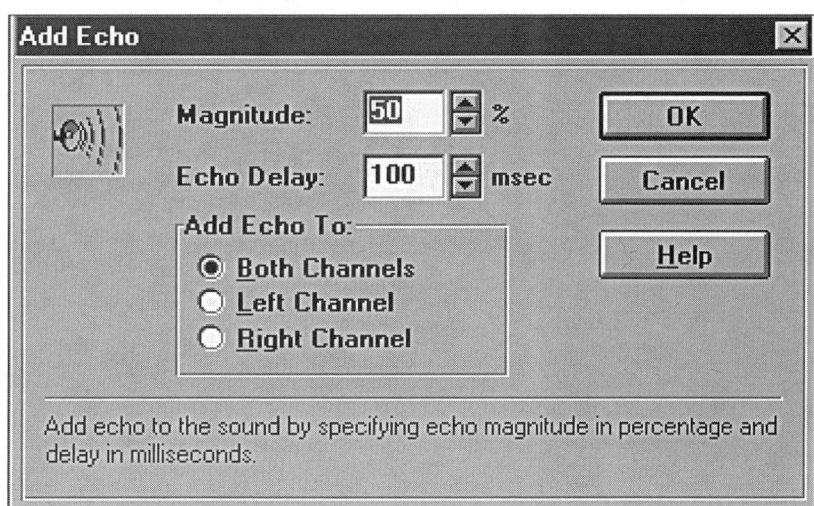

**Figure 4-14.**
Add Echo dialog

**3**   Delay sets the time between the original sound and its echo

**4**   Add Echo To lets you put the echo effect on either or both channels, if your file is stereo

**5**   Click on OK

## Invert Waveform

This flips the wave top-to-bottom for the entire high-lighted section of a file, for a subtle, but sometimes eerie effect. You can invert either or both channels of stereo files. To invert your waveform:

**1**   In the Edit window, select the waveform section you want to invert

**2**   Click on Invert Waveform from the Special menu for:

**3**   For stereo files, choose the channels to invert, then click on OK. That's it!

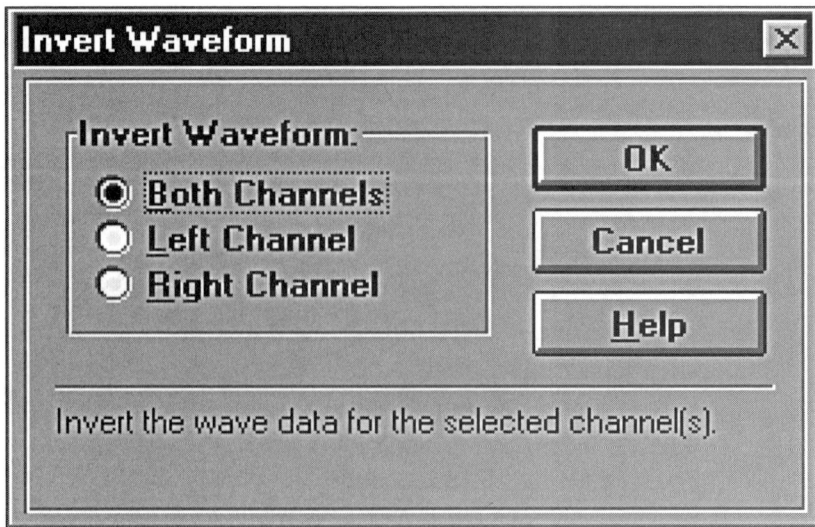

**Figure 4-15.**
Invert Waveform
dialog

## Rap!

Rap! is a one-step copy and insert; it causes a stammer-ing or staccato effect. To Rap! a file:

**1**    Highlight a section of the file in the Edit window

**2**    Click on Rap! from the Special menu; a copy the section you highlighted is inserted next to it.

## Insert Silence

This adds a section of silence before the selected section, the same duration as the selected section.

**1**    Highlight a section of the file in the Edit window

**2**    Click on Insert Silence from the Special menu

## Force to Silence

This replaces sound with silence in the selected audio section. You can silence either or both channels of stereo files.

**1**    Highlight a section of the file in the Edit window

**2**    Click on Force to Silence from the Special Menu. A box appears to let you select one or both channels.

**3**    For stereo files, choose the channels to silence, then click on OK

## Fade In/Out

Fades in or out of an entire or selected section of file by slowly raising or lowering the volume.

**1**   Click on Fade In or Fade Out from the Special
        menu for one of these boxes:

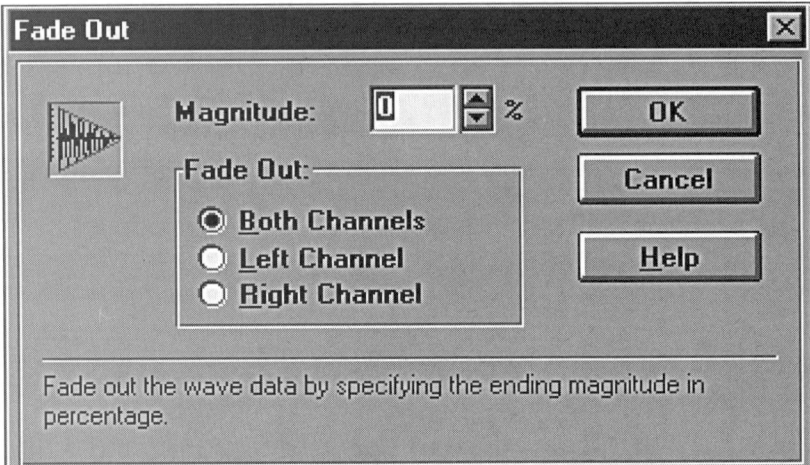

**Figure 4-16.**
Fade In dialog

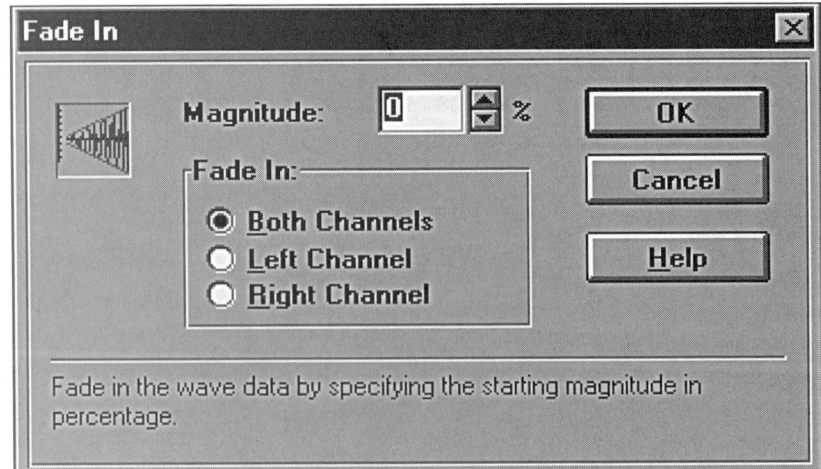

**Figure 4-17.**
Fade Out dialog

**2**   Type the magnitude (volume) of the fade you
        want in the Magnitude box. Fade In starts from
        your chosen starting magnitude to 100 percent.
        Fade Out begins at 100 percent and ends at
        your selected magnitude.

**3**   For stereo files, choose the channels to fade,
        then click on OK

## Swap

For stereo files, you can switch channels for entire files or selected sections. To use this feature, just click on Swap Channels from the Special menu.

## Pan Left to Right/Pan Right to Left

For stereo files, you can create the effect of a sound source moving from left to right or right to left. It's like you were turning the balance control back and forth.

First, select the waveform section you want to pan, then just click on Pan Left to Right or Pan Right to Left on the Special menu. That's it!

## Phase Shift

For stereo files, you can delay playback of one or both channels of the entire file or selected segment.

**1**   Click on Phase Shift from the Special menu for:

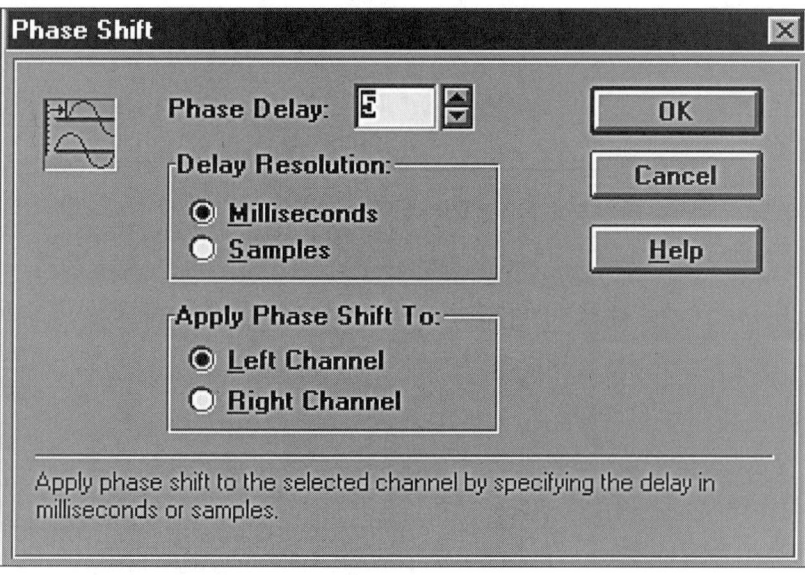

**Figure 4-18.**

**2**   Type the length of the delay in the Phase Delay box; you can also use the scroll arrows to increase or decrease the delay.

**3**   Select your Delay Resolution measurement by clicking on either Milliseconds or Samples. For example, to create a phase delay of 10 and resolution in Samples and a sample rate of 44,100/second, your delay would be 10/44,100 second, or 1/4,410 second. That's about 2.5 milliseconds.

**4**   Decide which channel to Apply Phase Shift to (left or right). In other words, which channel do you want to delay?

**5**   Click on OK when you finish

## Convert Format

Convert files between 8-bit, 16-bit, monaural and stereo, and 8-bit and 16-bit frequencies. Converting files can be a complex and time-consuming task, especially for larger files. To convert files, follow these steps:

**1**   Click on Convert Format from the Special menu for this dialog (see figure 4-19 on page 87): this is the same dialog as Record Settings, but for a file that already exists.

**2**   Click on Mono or Stereo Channels. If you convert from mono to stereo, the sound content of both channels will be the same. If you convert from stereo to mono, the original channels will be mixed together into one.

**3**   Select a sampling rate (bigger sounds better, but takes more space to store). If you select a smaller sampling rate than the existing one, you will

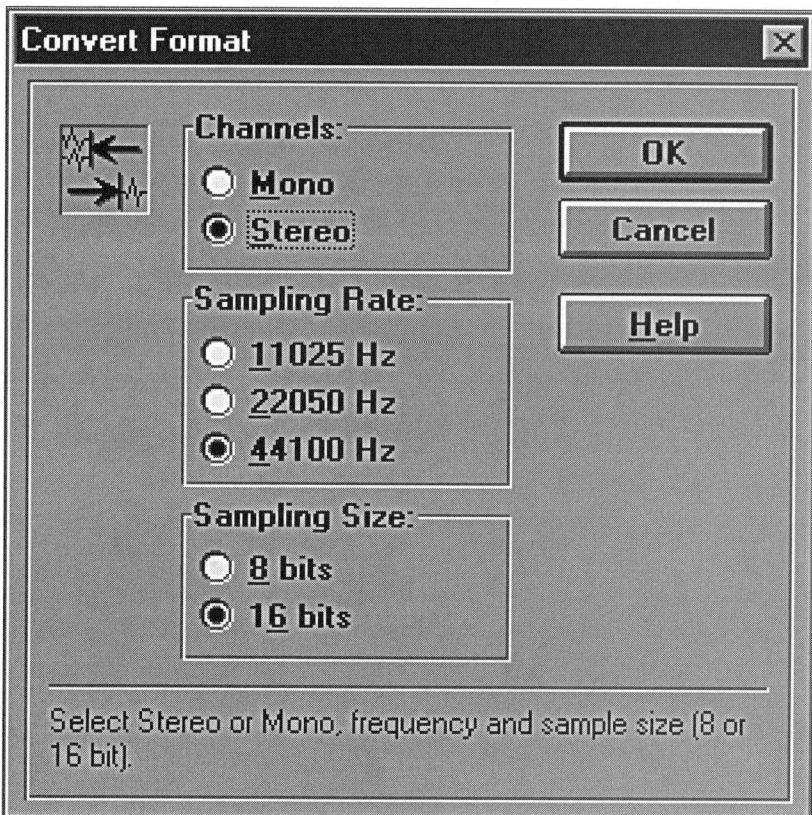

**Figure 4-19.**
Convert Format
dialog

permanently reduce the quality of the audio. If
you increase the sampling rate, the original
sound will still be the lower quality it was before.

4   Select a sampling size (again, bigger sounds
    better, but takes more space to store).

5   Click on OK when you finish

## Modify Frequency

This changes the playback rate of the entire file to either
11 kHz, 22 kHz, or 44 kHz. Changing to a lower frequency
slows down the playback speed by the same factor. A higher
frequency speeds up the sound in the same way.

You can only modify your file from its original sampling rate; you can't speed up a 44 Khz file or slow down an 11 Khz file. If you want to do that, first do a Convert Format on the file, as I just described.

For example, if your original file was recorded at 22Khz, changing it to 11 kHz cuts its play speed in half; changing it to 44 kHz doubles the speed (and the pitch of all the sounds). The entire file is changed to the new speed.

**1**    Click on Modify Frequency from the Special menu for its box:

**2**    Click on the new frequency

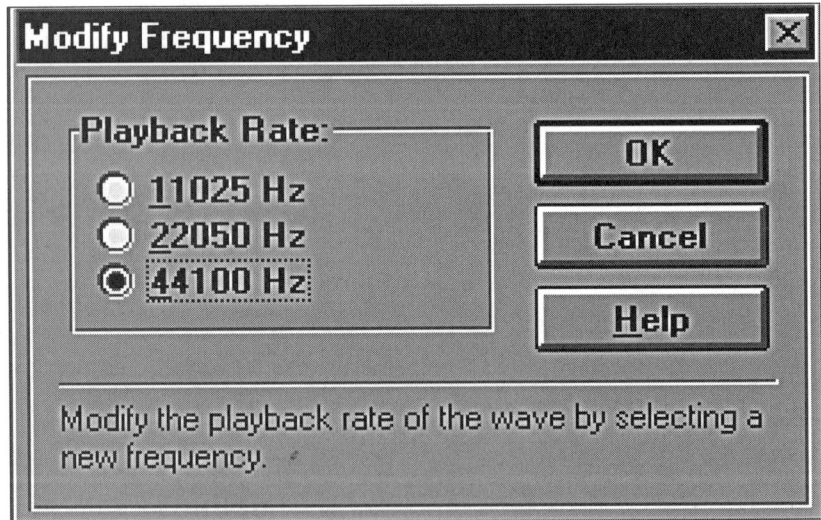

**Figure 4-20.**
Modify Frequency
dialog

**3**    Click on OK when you finish

## Amplify volume

This feature lets you increase or decrease the volume of the entire file or a selected section.

**1**    Click on Amplify Volume from the Special menu for:

**2** Select the amount (Magnitude) of the volume change. (Values less than 100% will decrease the volume.) Select the channels to be affected by the volume change: both, left, or right.

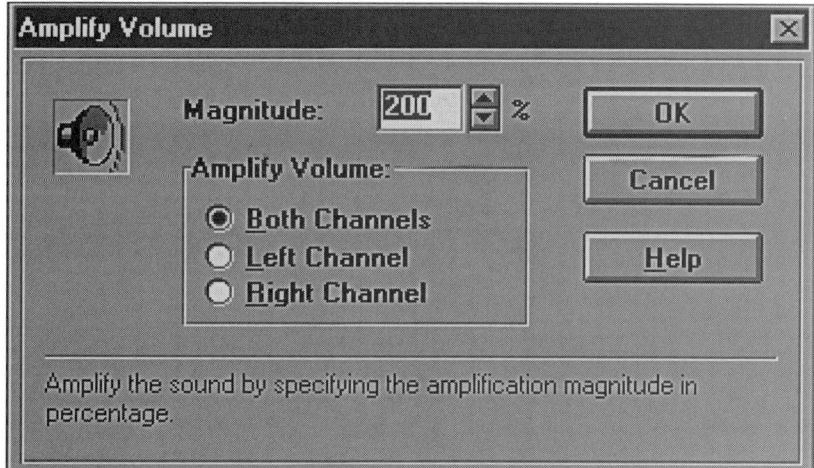

**Figure 4-21.**
Amplify Volume
dialog

**3** Click on OK when you finish

# WaveStudio Options

The Options menu lets you set defaults for recording, Creative Mixer, and display color

## Recording Settings

You can set the default record settings by clicking on Record Settings from the Options menu.

**1** From the dialog, click on your channels, sampling rate, and sampling size choices

This dialog looks very much like the Convert Format dialog in Figure 4-19. But Convert Format affects only the selected file while Record Settings changes all future recordings.

(This is the same box as I showed you in Figure 4-7.)

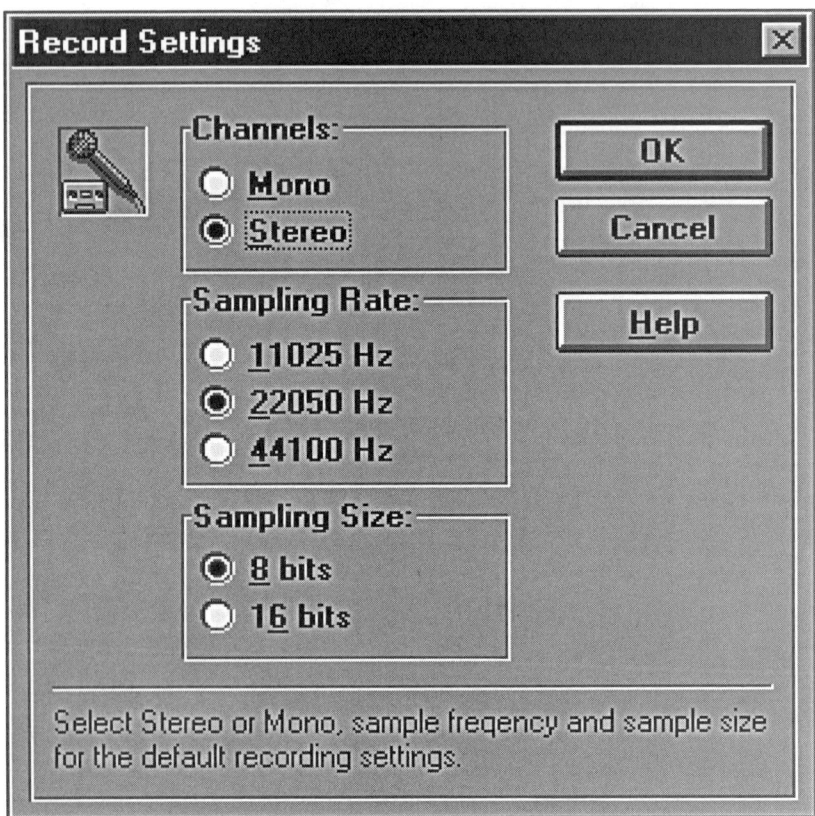

**Figure 4-22.**
Record Settings
dialog

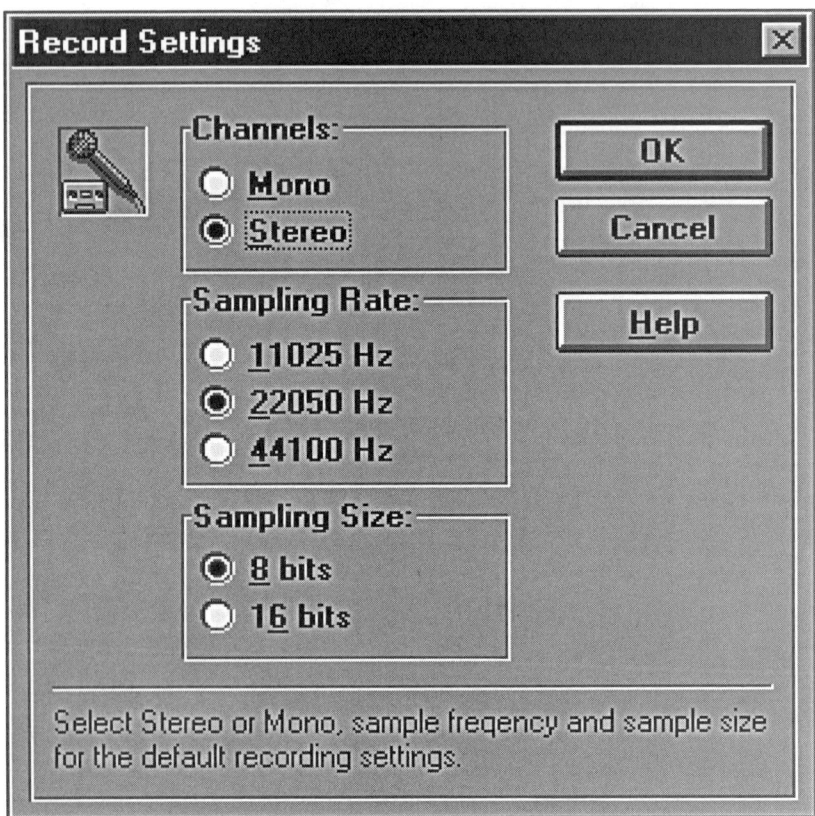

> **2**  Click on OK when you finish.

## Mixer Settings

Click on Mixer Settings from the Options menu to pop up the Creative Mixer application, described in Chapter 3.

## Customize Colors

You can change the colors WaveStudio uses for various display features by selection Customize Colors from the Options menu.

To change the colors, follow these steps:

**1** Click on any of the nine buttons to select colors for Edit window and Preview window features.

**Figure 4-23.**
Customize Colors
dialog

**2** From the drop-down color box, select the colors you like. Be careful to avoid two colors that

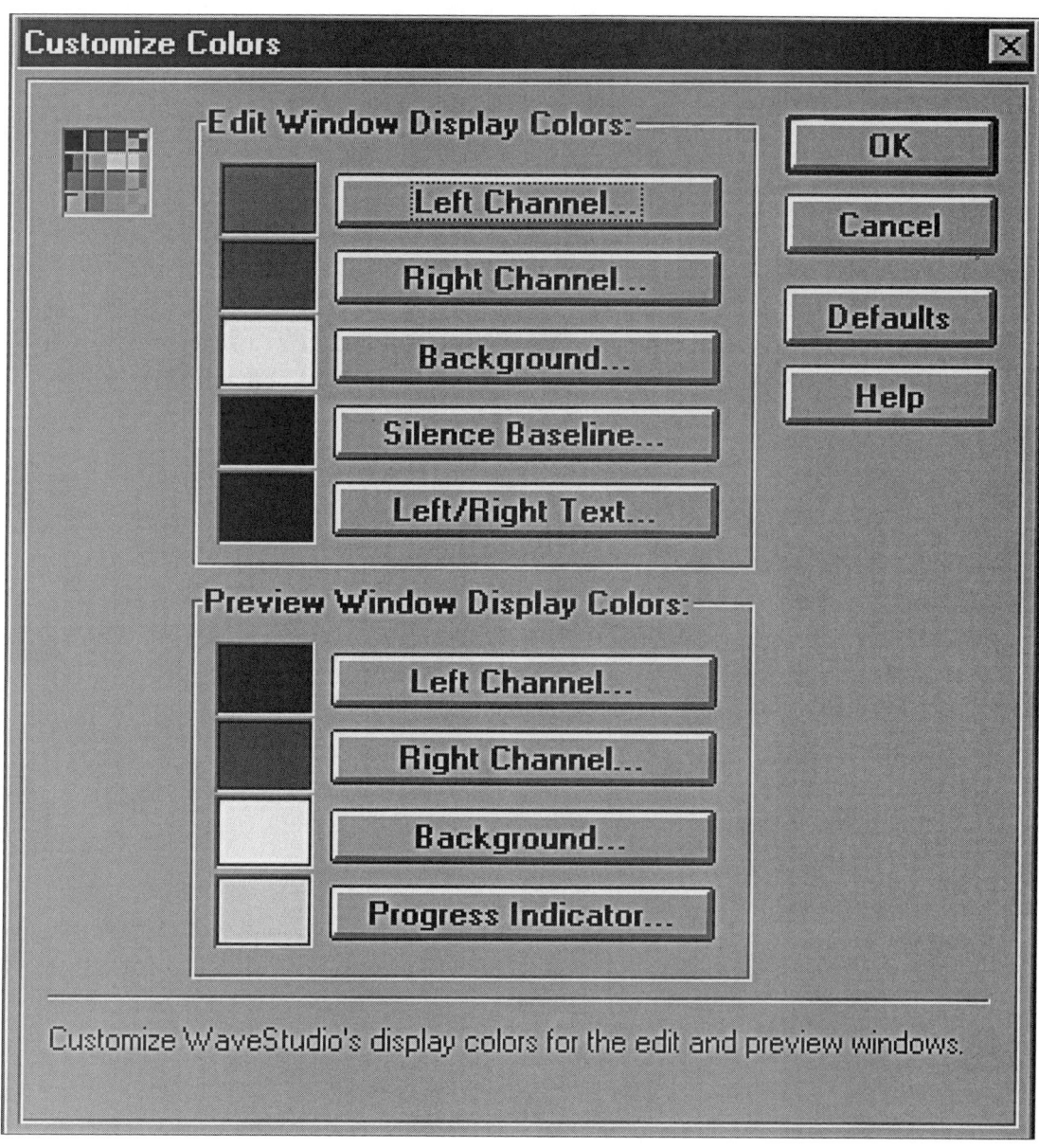

cancel each other. For example, white letters on a white background wouldn't really be visible.

**3** Click on OK when you finish

# WaveStudio Help

I've already described the contents of the Help menu a bit earlier, and this is simply a review.

## Help Contents

This is a "hypertext" display of topics that more information is provided about. A single mouse click on any underlined word or phrase brings you another window with more details. You can search for key words by clicking on the Search button at top. (You can always get help by pressing the F1 function key.)

## Search for Information

This menu item lets you bypass the overall help contents and begin directly to search for a key word.

## System Information

In this box, you get some selected information about your system: your Windows version and mode, the processor, available RAM and hard disk space.

## About

Here's the last parting word from your sponsors at Creative Labs: a little scrolling box of all the contributors to the product and a short musical riff to top it off.

WaveStudio is the jewel of the Creative Labs suite of applications for the Sound Blaster 16. It's complex, and

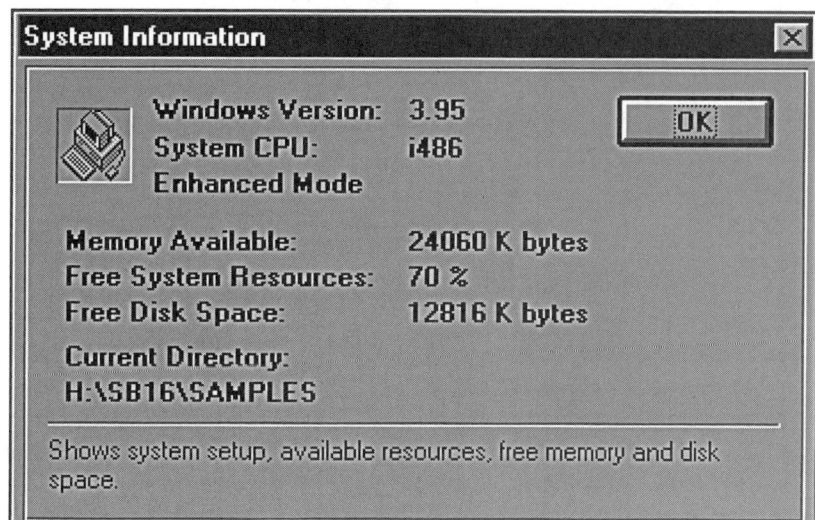

**Figure 4-24.**
System Information
box

rather complete. I hope my discussion has helped make it more fun and useful to you.

Next, a look at a specialized tool for integrating sounds into other Windows applications: Creative Soundo'LE.

# 5

# Creative Soundo'LE

Creative Soundo'LE is a special little tool from Creative Labs that lets you do *sound annotations.* You use it to record or select digital audio (WAVE) files and then place them directly into documents. For example, you might put a short sound note into a Microsoft Word letter; when the recipient opens your letter, they can play the sound back with a mouse click. Or, you might add voices and sound effects to a Microsoft PowerPoint presentation. When you're giving the presentation, you can click on the various slides to play the sounds.

## What is OLE?

Sound annotations are made possible using a built-in Microsoft Windows feature called OLE. This word stands for Object Linking and Embedding, and it's pronounced like the matador's call: olè. OLE is an automatic function to allow not only sound but other items such as graphics and even motion video to be placed in user files. Many applications, such as PowerPoint and Word for Windows, are designed to take advantage of OLE.

(OLE also expects that two Windows applets, called *Object Packager* and *Media Player* be available on your PC. The regular Windows installation puts them in the Accessories program group. And of course, you'll need a Sound Blaster 16 card and speakers on each PC for the sounds to be heard.)

One last term for you: an application that accepts OLE files is called a *client* (for obvious reasons). Only applications that are OLE clients can make use of Soundo'LE.

For more on OLE, you can read the Microsoft Windows reference documents that may have been provided with your PC. Or you can find many other books that discuss it.

Let's see how easy it is to use Soundo'LE and OLE.

# Starting Soundo'LE

To launch Soundo'LE, just double-click with your mouse pointer on its icon in the Sound Blaster 16 program group, shown here:

**Figure 5-1.**
Sound Blaster 16
program group

You now see the main window for Soundo'LE, shown below:

**Figure 5-2.**
Soundo'LE main
window

As you can tell, this appears very much like a stereo component front panel, perhaps for a tape recorder. The main features are a command bar at top, a graphic sound level "meter" in the middle, and transport control buttons at the bottom. At the right is a microphone/speaker icon.

Soon, I'll explain how to actually use OLE for embedding in or linking to your documents. But first, a tour of Soundo'LE's front panel. (You'll notice that this application is so simple it has neither a Toolbar nor a Help command.)

## Soundo'LE Command Menu

To access Soundo'LE's commands, you can use either the mouse or keyboard. Simply click the mouse pointer on a menu bar item at the top of the panel, then click again on the item you want on the menu that drops down. Or, you can hold the Alt key down while typing the underlined letter of the commands you want. For example, to open an existing sound file, type Alt/F, then O.

**Figure 5-3.**
Soundo'LE menu bar
with title bar

Here's the Menu bar area:

Four menu groups are visible on the Menu bar. They are:

- File      new/open/save/save as commands
- Edit      Copy sound as an object

⬤  Options  Wave info/Mixer settings/Recording
             settings/Always On Top

⬤  About    About Soundo'LE

Now for all the details:

## File Menu

| Table 5-1 | File Menu Commands |
|-----------|---------------------|
| **Command** | **Action** |
| New | Clears the Soundo'LE of any existing files |
| Open | Opens an existing WAVE file |
| Save | Saves the active file under its original name |
| Save As | Saves the active Edit window with a new name |
| Exit | Quits Soundo'LE |
| 1--4 | The most-recently opened four open files are listed at the bottom of the File list; to open one, click on the file name |

## Edit Menu

| Table 5-2. Edit Menu Command | |
|------------------------------|---|
| **Command** | **Action** |
| Copy Sound as an Object | Put the current WAVE file contents on the Clipboard |

## Options Menu

**Table 5-3.** Options Menu Commands

| Command | Action |
|---------|--------|
| Wave Info | Displays an info-box about current file settings |
| Mixer Settings | Pops up Creative Mixer applet |
| Recorder Settings | Pops up recorder settings dialog box |
| Always On Top | Forces Soundo'LE window to be above all others |

## About Menu

**Table 5-4.** About Menu Command

| Command | Action |
|---------|--------|
| About Soundo'LE | Scrolling info-box about developers |

# Soundo'LE's Transport Controls

Now let's take a look at the transport control group, at the bottom of the window. Use your mouse to click on these like tape-recorder push-button controls to control

**Figure 5-4.**
Soundo'LE transport controls

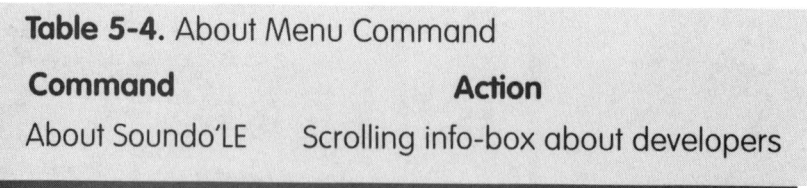

recording and playback.

Just for good measure, here's a table of the transport control actions:

**Table 5-5.** Soundo'LE transport controls

| Command | Action |
|---------|--------|
| Play | Plays the loaded sound file |
| Pause | Pauses playback of the loaded file. To restart, click again on Pause or on Play |
| Reverse | Moves the play position toward the beginning of the file, one small step each time you click |
| Forward | Moves the play position toward the end of the file, one small step at a time |
| Stop | Stops playing the loaded file; doesn't move the play position |
| Record | Records a new sound file |

*You can also use the Tab key to move to a Toolbar icon, then press the Spacebar to select it.*

# Opening Existing Sound Files

Soundo'LE plays and records only WAVE files—sound files with a file extension of .WAV. To open a file:

1. Click on File/Open for the File Open dialog box in Figure 5-5 on page 102.

2. Click on the file you want from the File Name list, then click on OK (or double-click on that file name). The file name shows up on Soundo'LE's title bar.

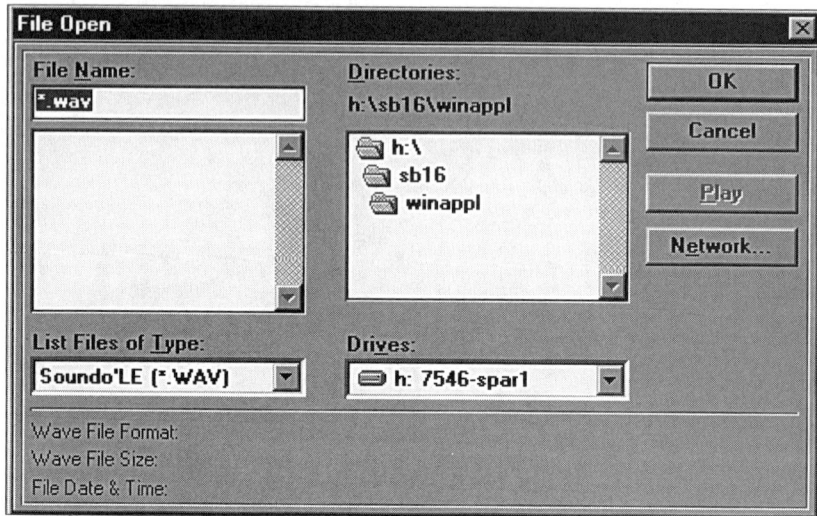

**Figure 5-5.**
Soundo'LE File Open
dialog

# Playing Sound Files

After opening your wave file, click on the Play button to begin hearing it through the Sound Blaster 16 audio system. You can pause or stop recording by clicking on the appropriate transport buttons. If you want to check the kind of file you've opened, click on the command Options/Wave Info to see this box, showing the recording settings that were used:

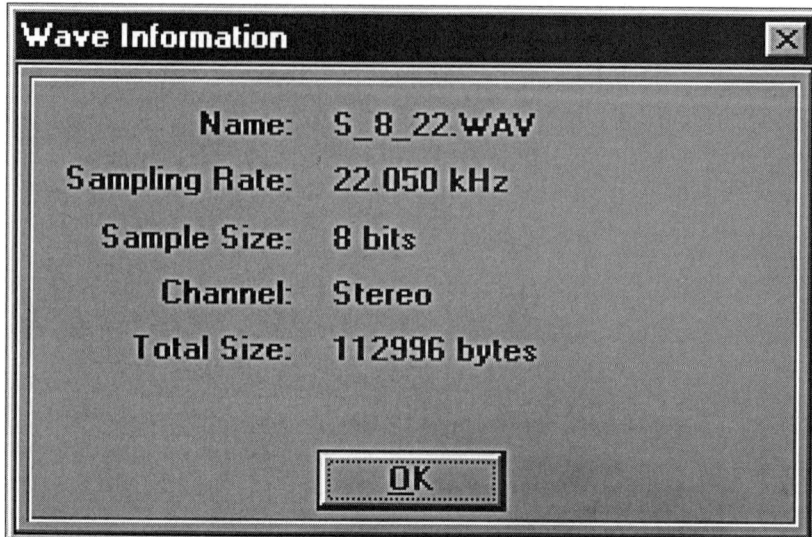

**Figure 5-6.**
Soundo'LE Wave Info
info box

# Recording Sound Files

You can make recordings from these three sources:

- A dynamic microphone plugged into the Microphone In jack on the Sound Blaster 16

- Line In (preamplifier level) audio from a cassette player, external audio CD player or the like, plugged into the Line In jack on the Sound Blaster 16

- Audio CDs played on your internal CD-ROM drive (optional)

To record a sound file:

**1**   Click on File, then click on New. If there's a file currently loaded (or one you've just recorded), you'll get a request to save it. Otherwise, Soundo'LE will simply clear out the old file and its Title Bar label.

**2**   Choose Recording Settings from the Options menu to get this dialog box:

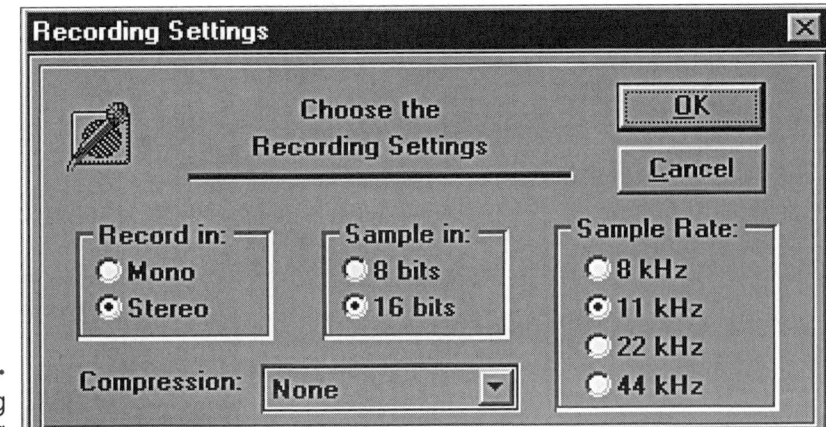

**Figure 5-7.**
Soundo'LE Recording
Settings dialog

**3**    Choose your settings according to the kind of audio source and audio quality you expect. Remember that these settings affect the size of your WAVE file. Table 5-6 explains these choices.

**Table 5-6.** Recording Settings Options

| Type | Option | Purpose |
|---|---|---|
| Record In: | Mono | Single-channel source (such as a microphone) |
| | Stereo | Dual-channel source |
| Sample In Options: | 8-bits | Low-quality recording |
| | 16-bits | High-quality recording |
| Sample Rate: | 11 kHz | Recording voice-quality |
| | 22 kHz | Recording voices or low-quality music; comparable to AM radio |
| | 4 kHz | High-quality recordings; almost CD audio quality, when combined with a 16-bit sampling rate |
| Compression: | None | no reduction of WAVE file size |
| | ADPCM | Compressing 16-bit files with Adaptive Differential Pulse Code Modulation. The compression ratio is 4:1 for 16-bit files and 2:1 for 8-bit files. |
| | CCITT A-Law | Compressing files according to CCITT standards. Compression ratio is 2:1. |
| | CCITT μ-Law | Compressing files according to CCITT standards. Compression ratio is also 2:1; slightly different audio quality from A-Law (experiment!) |

4   Click on OK when you're done to return to the
    Soundo'LE main window.

5   Open Creative Mixer by clicking on Mixer
    Settings from the Options menu (refer to
    Chapter 4).

6   If you need to, set up the input source, using
    EnsembleAV; refer to Chapters 2 and 3.

7   Click on the transport Record button

8   To monitor your recording progress, this
    info-box pops into view:

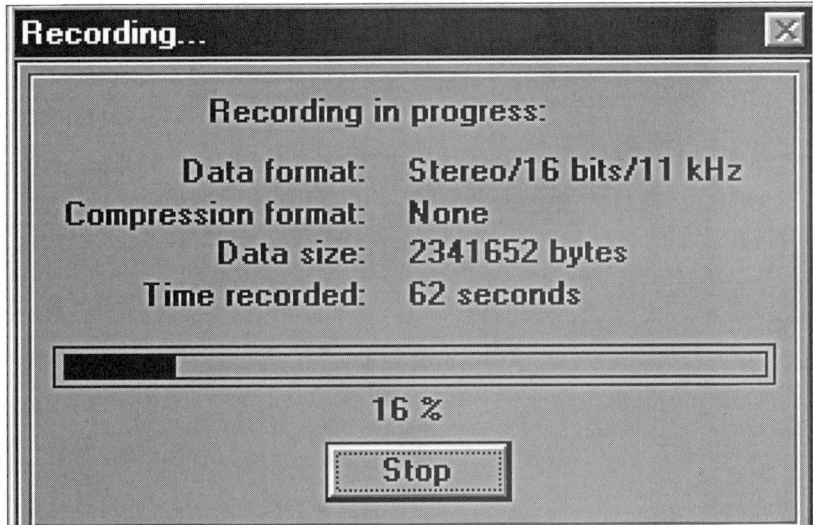

**Figure 5-8.**
Soundo'LE Recording
progress info box

You can also monitor the recording levels of your
audio sources on the bars at the middle of Soundo'LE's
window:

**Figure 5-9.**
Soundo'LE Recording
level bars

9   Click on the Stop button at the bottom of the
    Recording display box to stop recording

Your recording is saved on your PC's hard drive as a file. The size of your recording is limited only by the available disk space on your drive.

Remember that higher quality sound means recording at higher sample rates—and that larger settings will make for a larger file. For example, a stereo file is twice as large as a mono one, a 16-bit file is twice as large as an 8-bit file and a sampling rate of 44 kHz needs twice the space of a file recorded at 22 kHz. Multiply 2 x 2 x 2 and you get a file eight times larger than the more basic one. Yikes!

Be sure to select a hard disk with sufficient space and remove old unused files from your directories before recording.

## Saving a Sound File

To save your sound file, click on File, then Save. This dialog box appears:

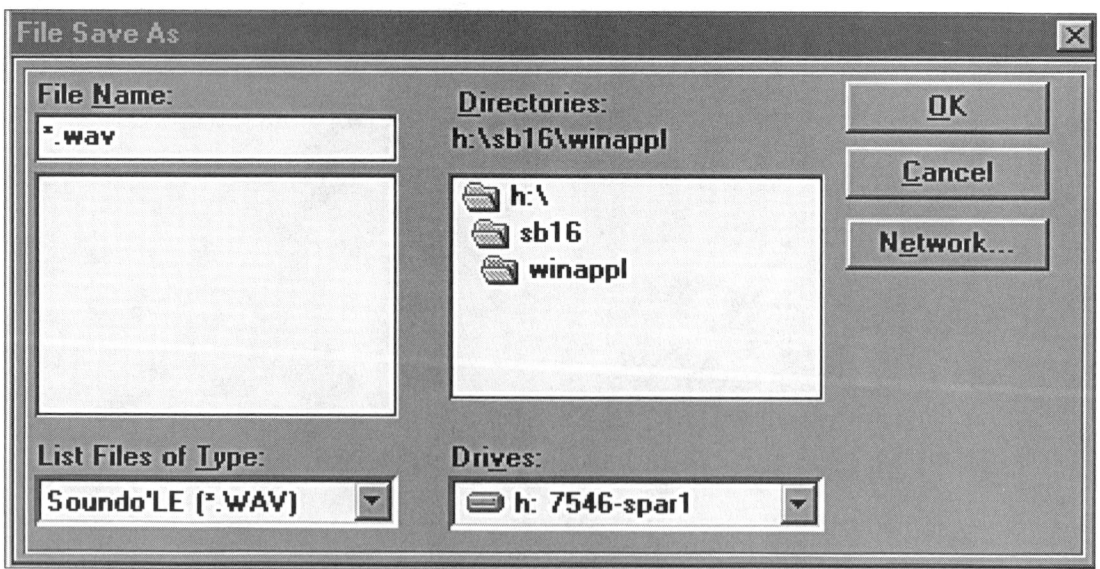

**Figure 5-10.**
Soundo'LE File Save
As dialog

Type the file name in the area shown. Also assign a Directory and Drive, or just accept the ones already shown.

# Linking and Embedding Sound Files

Here's how to use Soundo'LE to include your audio files in the document of a Windows application.

OLE gives you two distinct choices for including sounds in documents: linking or embedding. If you *embed* a sound in a document, a copy of the original sound file becomes part of the document. But if you *link* a sound file, only a reference to it is stored in the document—sort of a "sound bookmark."

If you update the original sound file it can't affect the copy in the embedded document. But, when somebody plays a linked sound in a document, it automatically "looks up" the current sound file, including the update. (That means that the original sound file also has to be available on your PC or network for the linked document to find.)

Remember, you can link or embed sound files only in applications that are OLE clients. Most newer Windows applications from major vendors do support OLE—especially those from Microsoft, Novell/WordPerfect and Lotus.

## Embedding from Soundo'LE

To embed a file using Soundo'LE, follow these steps:

1   Open or create a sound file using Soundo'LE, as I've already explained.

2   From the Soundo'LE File menu, click on Copy Sound As Object to copy the sound to the Clipboard. (The Clipboard is a Windows mechanism to temporarily hold audio, text, graphic or other information for use elsewhere. If you close Windows, anything on the Clipboard is lost.)

**3**     Launch the Windows application that has the document that you want the sound file in, and open the document.

**4**     Put the cursor at the point in the document where you want the sound to be heard.

**5**     While still in the Windows application with the document, click on Edit, then Paste. The sound is now copied from the Clipboard and included as a permanent part of the document file.

When the sound is embedded, this icon appears in the target document:

**Figure 5-11.**
Soundo'LE
microphone icon
(enlarged)

# Embedding from Within a Windows Application

To embed a file from inside the Windows application that created the document, follow these steps:

**1**     Start the Windows application and open the document that will accept the sound file.

**2**     Put the cursor in the document where you want to embed the sound.

**3**     Choose the applications menu command to embed an OLE object. For example, in Microsoft Word for Windows, click on Insert, then choose Object to get the dialog box, as shown in Figure 5-12. (Other applications may hide this command elsewhere.)

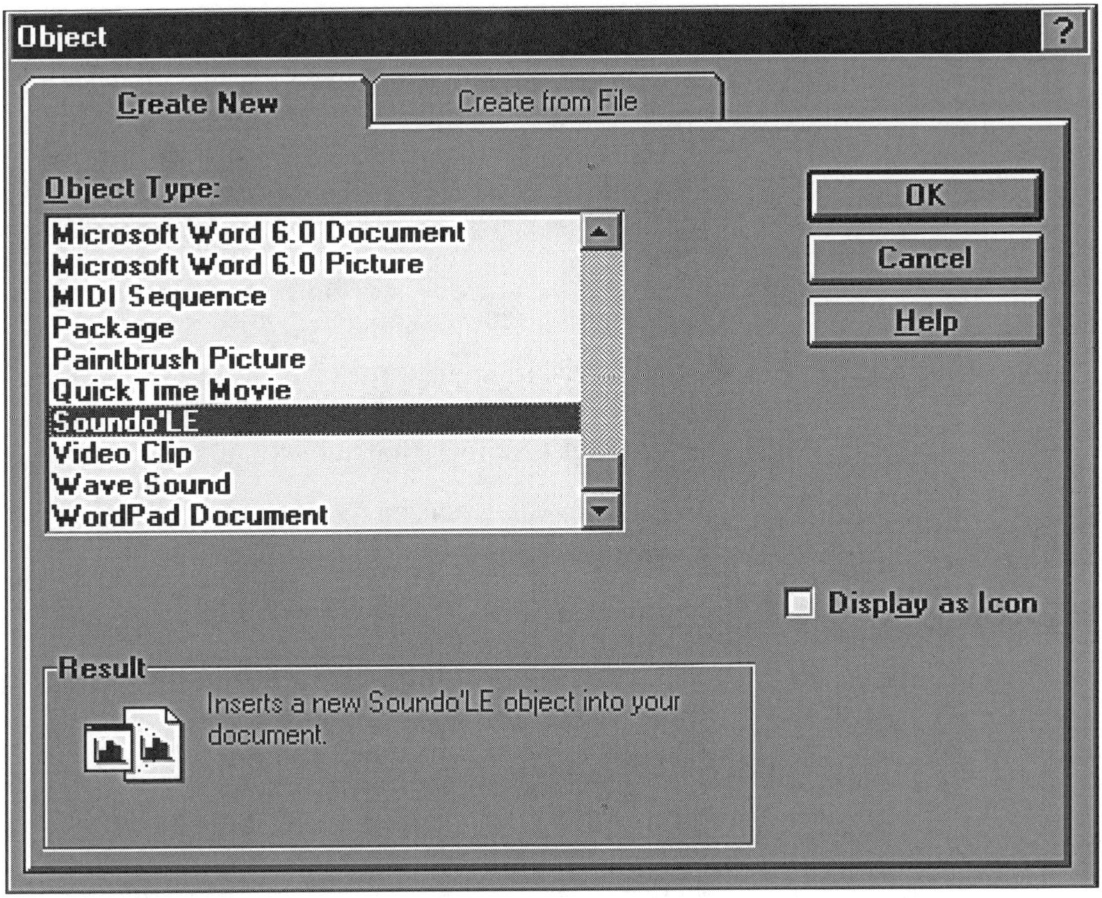

**Object**                                                                          ?

| **Create New** | Create from File |

**Object Type:**

Microsoft Word 6.0 Document
Microsoft Word 6.0 Picture
MIDI Sequence
Package
Paintbrush Picture
QuickTime Movie
Soundo'LE
Video Clip
Wave Sound
WordPad Document

OK
Cancel
Help

☐ Display as Icon

**Result**

Inserts a new Soundo'LE object into your document.

**Figure 5-12.**
Word for Windows 6
Insert Object dialog

**4**   In the Insert Object dialog, scroll to the Soundo'LE object type. Click on OK and Soundo'LE will be automatically launched, and its main window will appear.

*If Soundo'LE is not on the Object Type list, you must register Soundo'LE as an OLE application. Review Windows online help to find out how to use the Registration Information Editor, REGEDIT.EXE, which is usually in the Accessories program group.*

## Embedding using Drag-and-Drop

Here's a slick and quick way to use Soundo'LE to embed a sound file:

**1**    Open both Soundo'LE and the Windows application at the same time.

**2**    Arrange the windows of both applications so they are both visible. You can click on the Program Manager menu command Window, then click on Tile. Or, if you have Soundo'LE to be Always On Top, that will do nicely.

**3**    In Soundo'LE, open or record a sound file in the usual way.

**4**    Open a document in the target application.

**5**    Place the mouse pointer on the Soundo'LE icon on the right side of the Soundo'LE window. (That's the icon that looks like a microphone on top of a speaker grille.)

**6**    Hold down the mouse button and drag the icon to the position you want in the target document, then release the mouse button. That's it!

## Linking a Sound File

To link a sound file, you must first launch Soundo'LE. Follow these steps:

**1**    Using Soundo'LE, open or create a sound file in the usual way.

**2**    Click on Edit, then click on Copy Sound as Object to copy the sound to the Windows Clipboard.

**3**    Launch the application that has the document you want to link the sound file to.

**4** Open the document and place the cursor where you want the sound file to appear.

**5** Click on the application's Edit menu item, then click on Paste. The Soundo'LE icon now appears at the cursor position and the link has been created. (Remember, the sound file isn't actually a part of the document—there's only an "audio bookmark.")

## Playing a Linked or Embedded Sound

For any application that has a sound icon, simply double-click on it to play the embedded or linked sound file. If your sound player isn't already running, this will also launch Soundo'LE.

# Quitting Soundo'LE

Click on File, then Exit. If you changed a sound file and did not save it, you will be given a chance to save it now. Click on Yes to save, No to exit without saving, or Cancel to return to the Soundo'LE window.

Soundo'LE is a simple, yet handy tool to access the powerful Windows OLE features. You'll have a lot of fun with it.

Ever want your computer to tell you what's next in your busy day? Next is a little Creative Labs application called Creative Talking Scheduler. It does just that!

# 6

# Creative Mosaic: A Silly Game

t's the rage these days: package up a set of serious-minded applications and you feel the need to add levity. Creative Labs did it by throwing in this game: *Creative Mosaic.*

Does this game deserve a chapter of its own? Not really, but it doesn't belong anywhere else. It's not essentially an audio product, although it does play a tiny bit of music; and it doesn't use a synthesized voice either. (Finally, don't confuse it with the celebrated INTERNET Web browser by the same name.)

Creative Mosaic is a kid's game; a Windows-based version of the one you can buy for a buck at the toy store. The object is to slide tiles around until you get a number series or pieces of a picture in proper order.

Mosaic is in the *Sound Blaster 16* program group. To start Mosaic, click on its icon, and it appears:

**Figure 6-1.**
Creative Mosaic

You'll notice a set of cute icons at the top of this window. There's an ignition key, an ear and a figure going out the door. Click the key with your mouse, and you get a re-start for the game (the pieces are re-shuffled), and the sound of a car starting up. Click the ear, and a finger is inserted, while all sounds are muted. Go "out the door" and the game closes, while a little saccharine musical riff plays.

This option of the game board is the most simple: a three-by-three number matrix. A counter at top right keeps track of the number of moves you take—incredible stress. Now, let's go for broke.

Here's a more complex 5 x 5 matrix, with a picture instead of numbers:

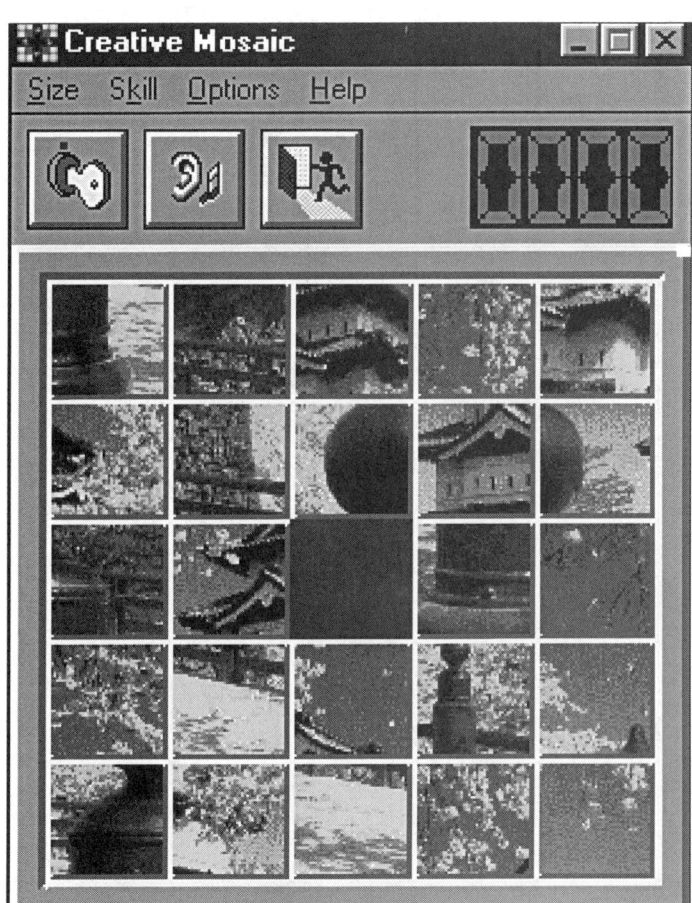

**Figure 6-2.**
Creative Mosaic
picture game: 5x5

Finally, a high-density 8 x 8 matrix, with a more abstract picture:

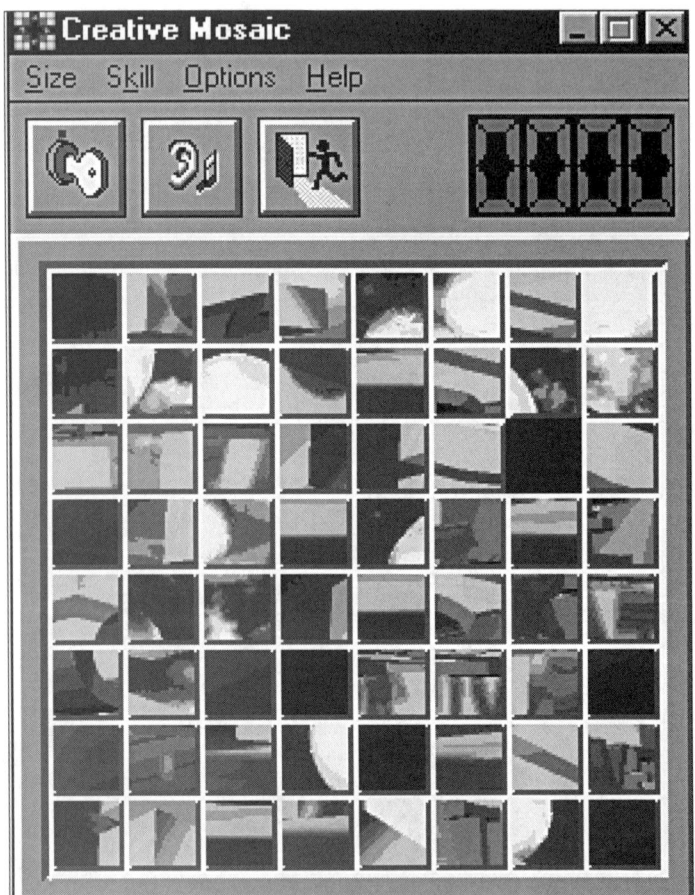

**Figure 6-3.**
Creative Mosaic
picture game: 8x8

I would bet there's a musical "payoff" for those who successfully solve the puzzle and make the picture visible. Alas, I didn't have the brute patience. You're on your own, dear reader.

# 7

# Creative Text-To-Speech Applications

**T**he world has been waiting for a talking computer for decades, it seems. Creative Labs has put together a group of coordinated applications that at least give your computer a voice. It's a monotone sort of critter—the very sort of synthesized voice that entertains us still in '50s sci-fi movie re-runs. And it's the heart of the Text-to-Speech Application Group!

Don't expect to be stirred by 'ol Abe emoting the Gettysburg Address, or by Lady McBeth trying to get her "damned spot" (of blood) out. But there is value in the spoken word to remind you of schedules without the need to constantly monitor your PC. That's the mission of Creative Talking Scheduler.

Creative Labs provides two other applications that give your PC a voice that speaks random text: Monologue (the "voice") and Dictionary Manager (the "sound translator"). Because English is probably the most irregular language on Earth, many words don't sound the way they're spelled. The Dictionary Manager does its part by maintaining a list of "exception" words and their corrected pronunciation. Monologue can be attached to some text or a spreadsheet to "proofread" their content using a synthesized voice. More on these applications soon.

Voices created by these applications are synthesized and their audio processed by the Sound Blaster 16 board. That means you'll need one installed in your PC with some attached speakers if you want to hear voices. (Everyone does, don't they?)

If you installed your Sound Blaster 16 applications using the software on CD-ROM, two Windows program groups were automatically created. I showed you the Sound Blaster 16 Group in Chapter 2. And here's the other one; the Text-to-Speech Group (see Figure 7-1).

(If you installed from diskette, these text-to-speech applications are provided and installed separately from the other applications.)

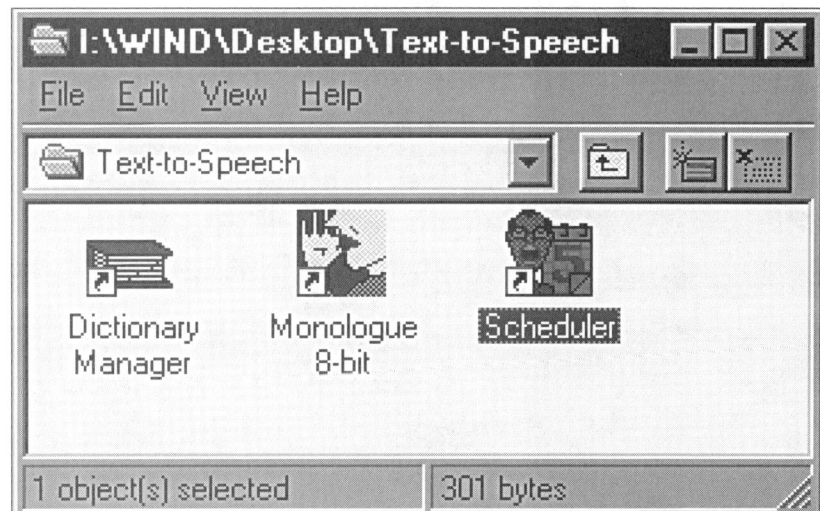

**Figure 7-1.**
The Text-to-Speech
program group

*If you'd prefer, you can combine the icons in this group with the Sound Blaster one. Simply click and hold the left mouse button on an icon, and drag it from one group to the other. When you release the button, the icon is permanently moved. You can then minimize and delete the empty group.*

# Starting Creative Talking Scheduler

To start Creative Talking Scheduler, click on its icon, shown in the group above. The first time you start, a message appears. Click on OK and the Talking Scheduler window pops onto the screen:

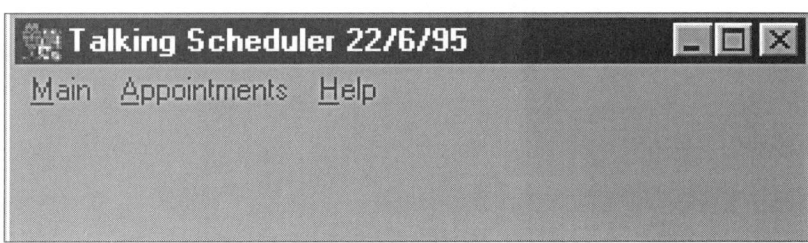

**Figure 7-2.**
Creative Talking
Scheduler application
window

You'll notice that Talking Schedule has a very simple application window. What you see at this stage is nothing but a launcher for other "daughter" windows. Only three commands are visible on the command line, and no toolbar or other icons.

As usual, you access the command menu by holding the [Alt] key down while typing the underlined character of the key word. Or, you can click on the word with your mouse. Either method displays a drop-down sub-menu for each main command.

Let's briefly review what's provided for commands.

## Main Menu

**Table 7-1.** Main Menu Commands

| Command | Action |
| --- | --- |
| SetUp | Voice setups |
| Clock | Pops up the Windows clock |
| Run | "Runs" Talking Schedule (minimizes it) |
| Exit | Exits Talking Schedule |

## Appointments Menu

**Table 7-2.** Appointments Menu Commands

| Command | Action |
| --- | --- |
| Review | Displays an info-box about current file settings |
| Add/Modify | Pops up Creative Mixer applet |
| Delete Days | Pops up recorder settings dialog box |

## Help Menu

| Table 7-3. Help Menu Commands | |
|---|---|
| **Command** | **Action** |
| Help Index | Just what you'd expect |
| About | A scrolling info-box listing the development crew |

## Setting up Talking Scheduler

Before using Talking Scheduler, you need to make a few setup choices. Ordinarily, you only do this once. Click the command Main/SetUp, for this dialog box, titled Program Defaults:

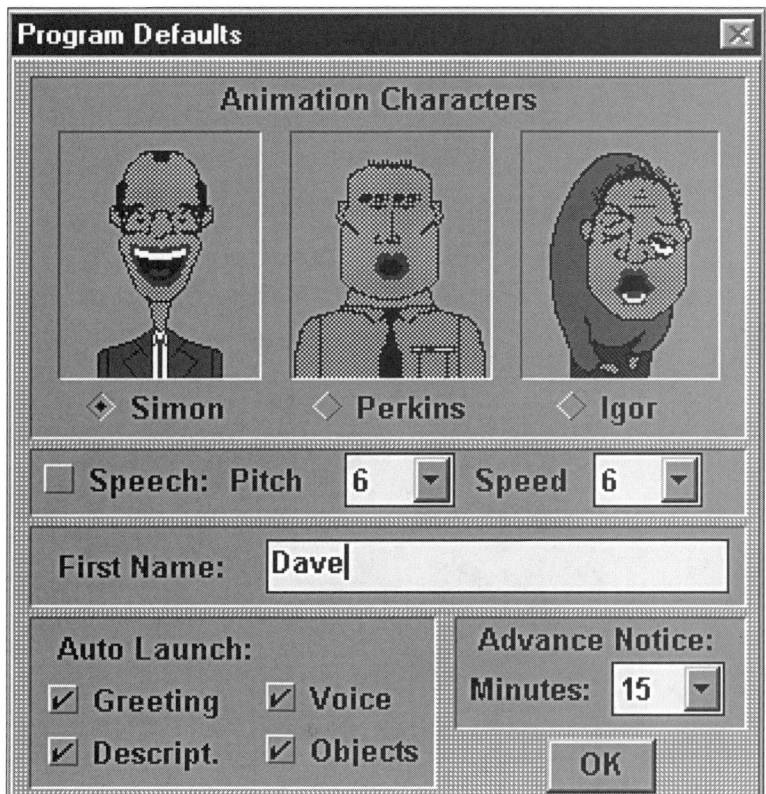

**Figure 7-3.**
Talking Scheduler
Program Defaults
dialog

These are the options you select in this box:

**Animation Characters**   Pick the cartoon character—Simon, Perkins or Igor—who will pop up to alert you about appointments. (Igor is an endearing character reminiscent of the Hunchback of Notre Dame.)

**Speech**   Click here to test the sound of each cartoon's voice. You can change the sound character of your cartoon's voice in these ways:

• **Pitch**   Choose from 1-9, with 1 the lowest voice (like a basso) and 9 the highest voice (tenor)

• **Speed**   Choose from 1-9, with 1 the slowest talker and 9 the fastest

**First Name**   Enter your name, or some other memorable phrase—up to nineteen characters. Creative Talking Scheduler can now speak your name as part of its announcements. Feel free to be creative!

**Auto Launch**   This selects which items will automatically activate when any appointment becomes due:

• **Greeting**   A voice message with your name, appointment time and person with whom you're meeting. It will sound something like, "Dave, you have an appointment with Sam from ten to eleven."

• **Description**   More details of the appointment

• **Voice**   Plays a wave file you record and attach to an appointment. You can create a detailed voice-mail message in your own voice that plays when the appointment is due.

- **Objects**   A file (an OLE object) attached to an appointment. A file can be a memo, spreadsheet, or e-mail message, and it's activated or launched when the appointment is due.

*About OLE: This stands for Object Linking and Embedding. See Chapter 5 and my discussion of Creative Soundo'LE and some OLE features.*

**Advance Notice**   Sets the time that the appointment reminder leads the actual appointment. This gives you time to prepare or make your way to an appointment. You can set any time from zero to sixty minutes in five-minute increments.

Click on OK when you finish to close the setup window and return to the main window.

## Running Talking Scheduler

Once you've set up the Talking Scheduler feature options, it's ready to activate. (Of course, for any actual value, you'll also need to put in some schedule items. That's coming up.) To activate Talking Scheduler, click on the command **File/Run** to minimize it to an active program icon. Or, simply click the minimize box at top right (that's the one with the single underline bar in it).

Remember that Talking Scheduler must appear as an active minimized application in Windows, or it will not alert you of schedules. (An active application that's minimized shows as an icon at the *bottom* of your desktop; that's different from an icon that's simply in a program group. To add schedules, or make other changes, you can simply double-click the icon to return it to full-size and again access the command menu.

Also remember that Talking Scheduler depends on your PC's internal clock to trigger appointments. If the clock is not correct, neither will your alerts.

To start Talking Scheduler every time you start Windows, add its icon to the StartUp Window. Here's how:

**1** Open the Text-to-Speech program group and locate the Creative Talking Scheduler icon.

**2** Open the Startup program group. You can find it from the Windows Program Manager by selecting the Windows command and scrolling through the list of available windows.

**3** Hold the [Alt] key down, point to the Talking Scheduler icon and hold the left mouse button down as you drag the icon from the Text-to-Speech group to the Startup group. The Startup group will now contain a copy of the icon.

**Figure 7-4.**
Talking Scheduler Appointment dialog

# Setting an Appointment

If you want a reminder about a meeting, you have to tell Scheduler about it. To enter an appointment:

**1** Click on the Scheduler icon to restore it. Click on the **Appointments/Add/Modify** command. This Make Appointments calendar box pops up (see Figure 7-4).

**2** Select the date for your appointment by clicking the date in the calendar. Notice the scroll arrows at bottom left and right of the calendar. The current month's calendar is showing. If you need to display another month, scroll forward or backward using the left scroll arrows. If you need another year, use the right scroll arrows.

**3** Point your mouse cursor on the clock, on your appointment's starting time. Hold the left

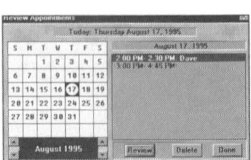

**Figure 7-5.**

mouse button down and drag the pointer to the end time. As you drag, a pie-shaped time "slice" fills the time period. When you reach the end time, release the mouse button; the time slice turns red. You can select create several appointments on the same clock. Appointments not selected appear in light blue.

Once you've placed the start time on the clock face, you can adjust both start and end times using the scroll arrows in the upper right corner of the box.

*Appointments must be at least fifteen minutes long. You may not overlap or double-book appointments. Appointments must start and on the same day. (For example, you can't enter a schedule item starting Tuesday at 11 p.m. and ending Wednesday at 1 a.m.)*

**4**   Type the name of the person you're meeting in the box labeled Person.

**5**   If you want to record a message, click on the Record button in the Annotated Voice area. More on that later.

**6**   If you want the system to read you a detailed reminder, type up to 127 characters describing your upcoming meeting in the box marked Appointment Description.

**7**   Click the buttons in the Auto Launch area to select the features you want automatically launched. You can also choose the "face" of the character who will make the announcement.

**8**   Repeat the clock-wipe process to add other appointments for this date, and click on the Done button when they're all entered. This returns you the Make Appointments calendar in Figure 7-4 on page 124. You can select more dates and more times until you're done.

**9** Minimize the Creative Talking Scheduler icon again, to enable any future announcements.

## Checking Appointments

To stay on track for your schedule, you'll want to review your appointments. Here's how:

**1** Restore Talking Scheduler by clicking on its minimized icon. Click on the command **Appointments/Review**; the current month's calendar appears. Any day with an entered appointment appears in red.

**2** Click on the date you want to check. Every appointment for the day appears in a listbox at right. Here's a review box for 17 August, 1995:

**Figure 7-6.**
Talking Scheduler
Review Appointments
dialog

*Special note: Are you wondering what's so important about 17 August? Well, that's my birthday. All gifts of value are cheerfully received—just send them to the Publisher care of me.* No live animals, please!

**3**   To view the details for a specific appointment, highlight it in the list and then click on the Review button. This box pops up:

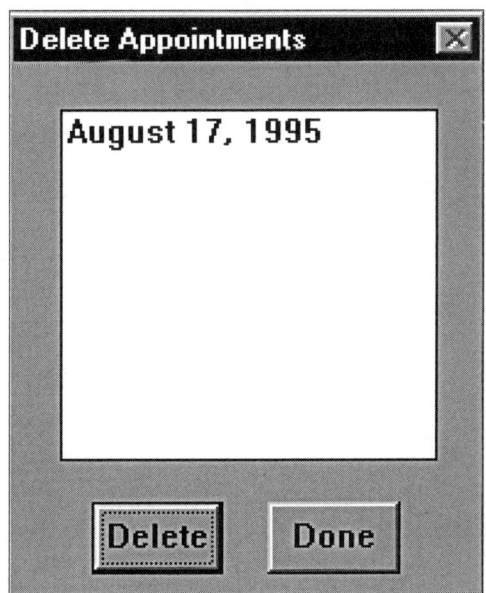

**Figure 7-7.**
Review (one)
appointment dialog

A synthesized voice announces the appointment and a box shows any OLE objects connected with it. An appointment description shows the appointment as you entered it.

**4**   To hear any attached voice message or stop playing it, use the Play and Stop buttons.

**5**   When you finish hearing and viewing the appointment, click on the Done button and then on the Review Appointments Done button to return to the main box. You'll now want to minimize Talking Scheduler to re-enable it.

## Changing an Appointment

It's just as easy to change a schedule as it is to make one. Here are the steps:

**1**   Restore Talking Scheduler and click on **Appointments/Add/Modify.** The calendar dialog box you saw in Figure 7-4 pops up.

**2**   Click on the date that has the appointment you want to change; the review box in Figure 7-6 on page 126 pops up.

**3**   Click to select the time slice for the particular appointment; the slice changes from blue to red.

**4**   Make your appointment changes; you can use the scroll buttons at top right to modify times.

**5**   When you finish, click on the Done button, then on the calendar Done button; finally minimize the Scheduler again.

## Canceling an Appointment

If you have to cancel a meeting, there are three ways to delete it from your calendar:

● Delete on the Appointment Clock, or

● Delete it from the Review Appointments dialog, or

● Delete appointments for a whole day with the Delete Days command. Now for the details.

## Delete Using Appointment Clock

**1**   Click on the Scheduler icon. Click on **Appointments/Add/Modify.** The Add/Modify calendar dialog pops up, as in Figure 7-4.

**2**   Click on the day that has the appointment you want to delete.

**3**   Click on the time slice inside the clock for the appointment you want to delete, then click on the Delete button.

**4**   When you finish, click on Done, and Done again on the calendar; finally minimize the Scheduler.

## Delete Using Review Appointments Dialog

**1**   Click on the Scheduler icon. Click on **Appointments/Review.** The Review Appointments dialog in Figure 7-6 pops up.

**2**   Click on the date of your appointment for the date window. Appointments for that day are on the right, as you saw in Figure 7-6.

**3**   Place the cursor on the appointment you want to delete, then click on the Delete button.

**4**   When you finish, click on Done, then Done on the calendar; last, minimize the Scheduler.

## Delete Using Delete Days

**1**   Click on the Scheduler icon. Click on Appointments, then Delete Days. The Delete Appointments dialog pops up.

2    Click on the date that you want to delete *all appointments* from, then click on the Delete button.

3    When you finish, click on Done; minimize the Scheduler again.

## Recording a Message with an Appointment

It's easy to attach a recorded message to an appointment, to give you more details than you get from your cartoon friends' synthesized voice. You will need a microphone plugged into the Microphone In jack on the Sound Blaster 16. To record a voice message with your appointment:

1    Click on the Scheduler icon. Click on **Appointments / Add/Modify.** The familiar Make Appointments calendar shown in Figure 7-4 on page 124 pops up.

2    Click on the date you want, and the Review Appointments box shown in Figure 7-6 on page 126 appears. Click on the time slice of your appointment or enter a new appointment.

3  With a particular appointment's time slice highlighted, click on the Record button and speak clearly into the mike; you can talk for as long as 30 seconds.

The Record Voice Annotation box appears:

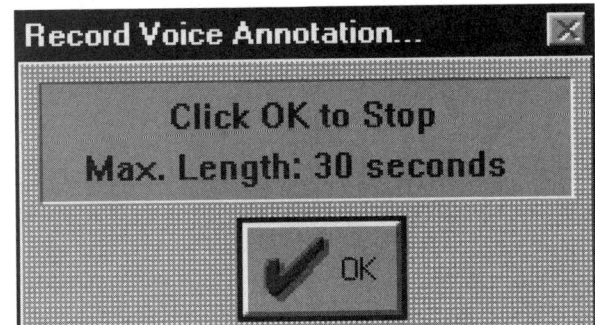

**Figure 7-8.**
Talking Scheduler
Record Voice
Annotation dialog

As you record, this window shows you the time remaining out of your 30-second allotment. (You'll want to delete any unneeded voice annotations to recover the disk space they use.)

4  When you finish, click on OK, then Done on the Appointments box, and Done on the Appointments calendar; finally, minimize the Scheduler.

5  To listen to a recording, click on Play in the Review Appointments box, instead of on Record.

## Attaching other elements to Appointments

You can attach a variety of other items to an appointment, and they are automatically launched or activated when the appointment becomes due. These items can be files, graphics, or sounds, and they are called OLE *objects*.

For a full discussion of OLE, and the meaning of embedding and linking, read Chapter 5, where I described it for Creative Soundo'LE. In brief, an *embedded* object is actually copied from the application that creates it to the application document that uses it. But for a *linked* object, only a reference to the object is placed in the application's document. Whenever the object is needed by the document or activity, it is located by using the stored reference.

## How to Embed

You can embed an object in an appointment two ways:

- Embed when the program that created the object is not open. You can embed a Word for Windows text document without even opening Word for Windows.

- You can paste when the object's program is open or you just need part of a file. You can link a Lotus file with the program and file on screen, or you can link just two columns of the spreadsheet to your appointment.

## The Embed Command

**1**    Click on the Scheduler icon. Click on **Appointments/Add/Modify**. The Make Appointments calendar (Figure 7-4) pops up.

**2**    Click on the date you want, then click on the time slice of your appointment or make a new appointment.

**3**    With the time slice selected, click on the Object menu item on the Toolbar, then click on Embed to show the Embed Object dialog shown in Figure 7-9.

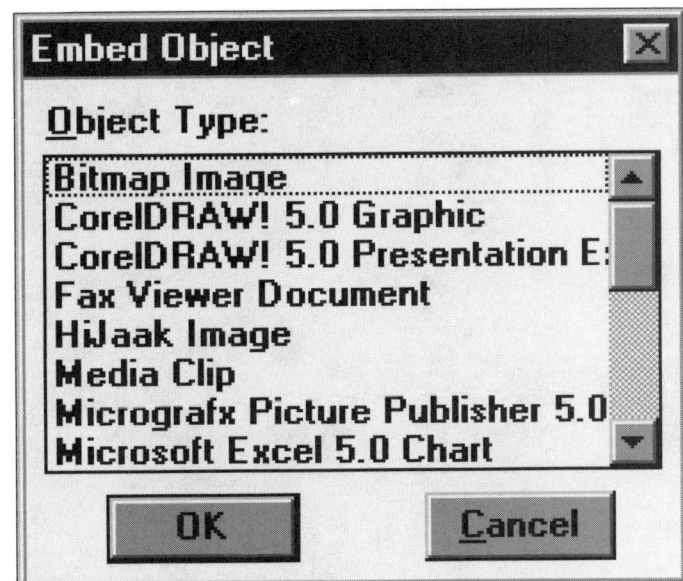

**Figure 7-9.**
Talking Scheduler
Embed Object dialog

4  Find the application with the object (file) you want to embed, by scrolling through the list. When you find the application, click on OK, and the application is launched. For this example, I chose Word for Windows, but I could have as easily selected a sound or graphics application.

5  Embedding a new file requires that you create the object. Then click on Update from the application's File menu. When you finish, exit the program.

6  Embedding an existing file requires that you open the file and exit the program. You'll see a message asking if you want to update the object; click on Yes.

7  When you finish, an icon appears on the OLE Object box of the Appointments window, as you see in Figure 7-11 on the following page.

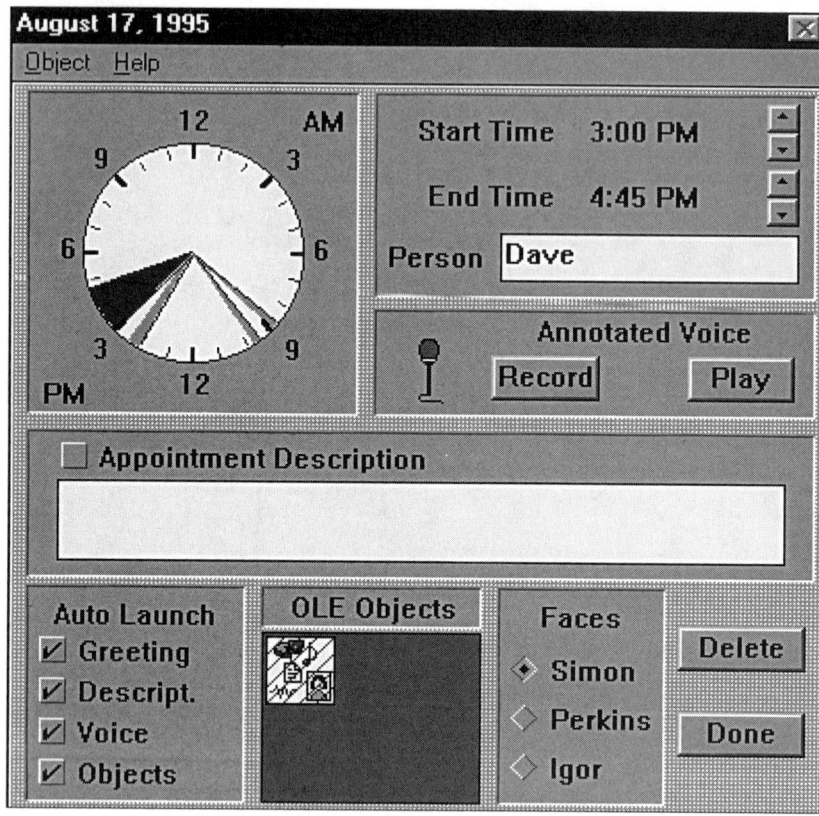

**Figure 7-10.**

Talking Scheduler
Appointments dialog
with embedded
object

This icon represents the embedded object—in this case, a Word for Windows text document.

## Embed and the Paste Command

1   Click on the application that has the file you want to embed. Open the file.

2   Highlight the portion of the file you want to embed, or select the whole file as your object.

3   Open Talking Scheduler. Click on **Appointments/Add/Modify.** The Make Appointments calendar window (Figure 7-4 on page 124) pops up.

**4** Click on the date you want, then (using the Appointment box shown in Figure 7-5), click on the time slice of your appointment or make a new appointment.

**5** Click on the Object menu item on the Toolbar, then click on Paste.

**6** When you finish, an icon appears on the OLE Object box of the **Add/Modify** window. This icon represents the embedded object, as in Figure 7-10 on page 134.

## How to Link

There is just one way to link a file to an appointment.

**1** Click on the application that has the file you want to link. Open the file.

**2** Highlight the portion of the file you want to link, or select the whole file as your object.

**3** Click on Edit, then click on Copy to copy the data to the clipboard.

**4** Open Talking Scheduler. Click on **Appointments/Add/Modify.** The Make Appointments calendar of Figure 7-4 pops up.

**5** Click on the date you want, then (Figure 7-5) click on the time slice of your appointment or make a new appointment.

**6** Click on the Object menu item on the Toolbar, then click on Paste Link.

**7** When you finish, an icon appears on the OLE Object box of the Appointments dialog, as in Figure 7-10 on page 134. This icon represents the embedded object.

## Detaching an Object

You can detach an item from an appointment; you can delete the attachment but keep the calendar entry. To detach an object from your appointment:

**1**    Open Talking Scheduler. Click on **Appointments/Add/Modify.** The Make Appointments calendar (Figure 7-4) pops up.

**2**    Click on the date you want, then click on the time slice of your appointment (in Figure 7-5).

**3**    To detach one OLE object from an appointment, select the icon in the OLE Object box of the file you want to detach. Click on Objects, then click on Clear and the icon disappears from the OLE box.

**4**    To detach all OLE objects from an appointment, click on Objects, then click on Clear All; all icons disappear from the OLE box.

## Quitting Creative Talking Scheduler

There are two ways to remove Scheduler from your Windows desktop session:

- Click on File, then click on Quit. This completely closes Creative Talking Scheduler.

- Click on File, then click on Run. This removes Scheduler from your screen but keeps it open to remind you of any appointments.

**Table 7-4.** Creative Talking Scheduler Menu Commands

| Menu | Description |
|---|---|
| SetUp | Shows defaults for Creative Talking Scheduler |
| Clock | Shows Windows clock |
| Run | Minimizes Creative Talking Scheduler to an icon |
| Quit | Exits Creative Talking Scheduler |

| Appointments Menu | Description |
|---|---|
| Review | Lists your appointments |
| Add/Modify | Lets you add or change appointments |
| Delete Days | Removes all appointments for a chosen date |

| Object Menu | Description |
|---|---|
| Paste | Attaches a copied object to an appointment. |
| Paste Link | Links all or part of a file to an appointment |
| Links | Shows current links to an appointment |
| Embed | Creates an object and attaches it to the appointment |
| Clear | Detaches one object from an appointment |
| Clear All | Detaches all objects from an appointment |
| Object | Lets you edit the chosen object |

| Help Menu | Description |
|---|---|
| All commands, buttons, and functions have on-line help providing information or directions about the selected topic. | |

# Monologue for Windows

It's robotic-sounding, it's monotone, but it's useful and attention-getting. Monologue for Windows is a synthesized voice that will read ordinary text or numbers aloud.

Besides parlor games and acts of techno-voodoo, what can Monologue do for you? Here are some possibilities:

- Have Monologue for Windows read your e-mail while you do something else (possibly sort the snail mail).

- Verify a spreadsheet or report visually as Monologue reads it aloud. This may save some associate a heap of boredom as you check the weekly payroll, for example. (Won't help you much, but that's life!)

- Let Monologue read a report aloud for proofing. Hearing the text can sometimes alert you to an error that is missed even after reading the same sentence a dozen times.

- Using Monologue, programmers can incorporate speech into their own Windows programs or even into macros inside shrink-wrapped Windows applications. You can set up macros to review spreadsheets or database programs to report on changes in selected cells or fields, for example.

- Using the Dictionary Manager, you can even allow for local preferences in pronunciation. If you say New York and your boss says New Yawk, you can save two sets of pronunciations for Monologue to use in different users' PCs.

## About Monologue

This section is a brief background of how Monologue for Windows works, if you have any interest in what goes on "under the hood." If you don't care, just skip ahead.

## How Monologue Recreates Speech

Monologue uses two methods for "remembering" how to pronounce words:

- **Rules-based speech generation** Keeps words stored only as sounds and converted into digital waves to create "speech."

- **Table-based speech generation** Keeps words stored as text and sound. Monologue searches the table for the text and "speaks" the sound.

- Monolog uses the rules-based method, until it comes to a word that's been put in the Dictionary Manager's list. The Dictionary Manager has a set of words that are often mispronounced or words with several or regional pronunciations. You can add your own words to the list or edit the "starter set."

## Where Monologue Finds What to Say

Monologue uses three sources for input. Each input source is called a *Mode* on the Monologue for Windows dialog (Figure 7-11 on page 140):

## Clipboard Mode

Clipboard is the default text source (and it's selected in the radiobutton in the figure). When you choose this mode, Monologue reads text it finds on the Windows Clipboard. You put text on the Clipboard by doing a

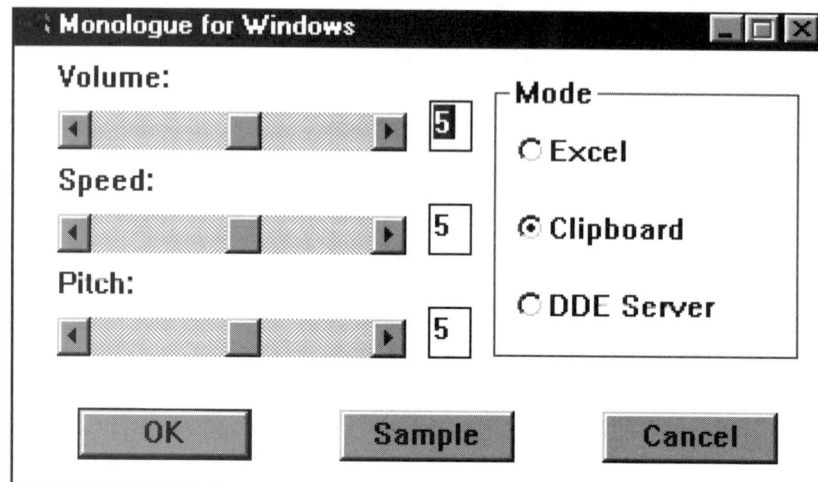

**Figure 7-11.**
Monologue for
Windows dialog, with
Mode on the right
side of the screen.

Copy or Cut from an application's text file. This lets you select any random text you please for Monologue to read. (Clipboard is only a temporary storage, and all information on it is lost when you close Windows.)

## Excel Mode

In Excel Mode, Monologue reads data directly from whatever cells are highlighted in an open Excel spreadsheet. Naturally, you must open the spreadsheet and highlight the cells you're interested in hearing.

## DDE Server

DDE Server mode is used by applications developers to provide a stream of text from an application directly to Monologue. To use this technique, you'll need to understand DDE and how to write macros using it. That's beyond the scope of this book.

*Two special notes: you can also use direct DLL calls to Monologue for Windows. This is a technique used strictly by programmers. Finally, you can use DDE or DLL techniques for your personal work, but if you want to distribute an application commercially, you'll need to buy a license. If this is you, contact Creative Labs for more details.*

# Starting Monologue for Windows

Double-click on the Monologue for Windows icon in the Text-to-Speech group, shown way back in Figure 7-1. The Monologue for Windows dialog box appears:

*If you find yourself using Monologue often, you can start it up whenever you start Windows by moving its icon to the special Windows Startup group. (Look back at my discussion for Talking Scheduler for details on how to do that.)*

# Testing Monologue for Windows

Before you try to Monologue, be sure the Sound Blaster 16 card is properly installed and there are some speakers (or a pair of headphones) connected. Also, you must be running Windows with *multi-media extensions*. If you've bought a pre-loaded multi-media computer, you're sure to have it.

Set Monologue up using these three steps:

**1**    Click on the Monologue for Windows icon to launch the application and open its dialog box.

**2**    Press the Sample button on the Monologue window. You should hear the phrase, "Testing. One, two, three." This is your built-in self-test.

# Minimizing Monologue

After opening Monologue for Windows, you can reduce it to an icon in one of two ways:

● Click on the minimize button: the downward arrow in the upper right corner of the screen; or

● Click on Minimize from the Monologue for Windows system menu.

## Making the PC Read Aloud: Converting Text to Speech

It's time to make your PC speak in a useful way. Recall that you can choose one of three *modes* or sources for text.

### Using Clipboard Mode

● Using any Windows application that displays text or number characters, first select the text you want to have read. (Ordinarily, you can simply drag the mouse pointer to highlight and select the text.) Then, use either the menu commands Edit/Cut or Edit/Copy to put the text on the Windows Clipboard.

● Move the mouse cursor to the minimized Monologue for Windows icon. Click the right mouse button and listen. You'll hear the text you've selected.

## DON'T ALWAYS BELIEVE WHAT YOU HEAR

Monologue for Windows doesn't always know how to pronounce punctuation. For example, an exclamation point (!) doesn't change the inflection of the playback. However, a question mark (?) does add an upward inflection in the sentence. Monologue can't recognize apostrophes, so it pronounces the word "it's" as "it ess," reading the sound of S spoken as a letter.

### Using Excel Mode

Excel mode is specifically for Excel users. First, select Excel Mode from the Monologue for Windows dialog. Next, start Excel, open the spreadsheet file, and highlight the text or figures you want to hear.

*Using Excel mode with other applications instead of Excel will probably give you gibberish.*

## Using DDE Mode

DDE mode is for use only with programs in which you have already built DDE links to Monologue for Windows. After selecting DDE Server Mode from the Monologue for Windows dialog, start your program with the linked macro or data, then run the macro or script that starts DDE "conversation."

## Programming with Monologue for Windows

You can add speech to the programs you already own, if they support DDE or DLL. You will need to look at a book discussing Windows programming to pursue this further. However, you should know the differences between DDE, macros, and DLL. I'll briefly review these strategies.

## DDE Interface

Monologue for Windows lets your application start ("initiate") a DDE conversation, sending data for Monologue to say aloud. The DDE server, within Windows, is the agent for your application, which acts as the DDE client. To start a conversation, the client supplies an application name and topic to the server. Monologue expects these to be MONOLOG and TALK, respectively. During the conversation, Monologue speaks any data it receives from the client. When the client finishes sending data, it sends a DDE terminate signal to the server, ending the session.

## Creating Macros

Many popular Windows applications include a macro language to automate complex tasks. You can build a macro to activate Monologue for Windows and speak selected text without actually clicking on the Monologue icon.

## DLL Interface

The DLL interface is the most elegant and efficient method of all to employ Monologue as a text-to-speech "engine." You can use Monologue as a resource (a "server") to any program that can support calls to external libraries.

Because the DLL call directly accesses Monologue's underlying functions, this technique uses a minimum of memory and Windows resources. The Monologue dialog box never even appears on-screen.

If you want to use DLL techniques, contact Creative Labs for more details and reference material for the DLL library of calls.

## Dictionary Manager

Dictionary Manager contains and controls an "exception dictionary"—a list of all the words that can't be properly pronounced by Monologue using standard rules. Here's what the Exception Dictionary looks like:

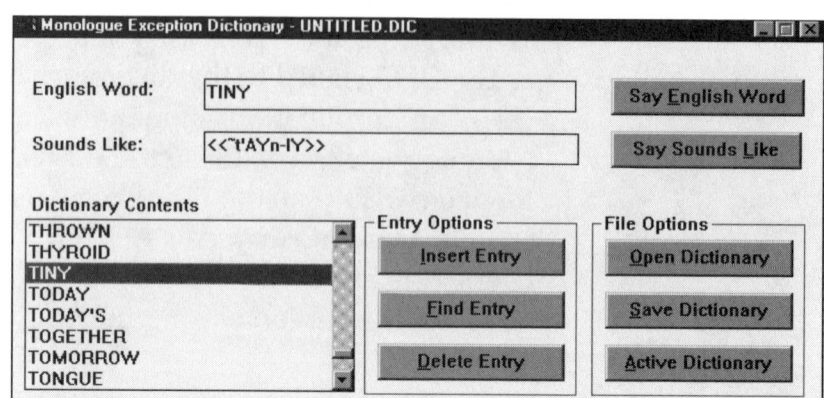

**Figure 7-12**

Monologue Exception Dictionary application window

Because English is not a consistent language to pronounce, the Exception Dictionary provides a large set of words that don't fit the "rules." You'll probably find more, and you can add them to the Dictionary as well.

To add a word to your Monologue vocabulary, use the Exception Dictionary dialog to add an entry and save it in a new dictionary. After creating new dictionaries, select which ones should be *active* for your Monologue for Windows sessions. The active dictionary selection remains in effect until you make another choice.

## Using Dictionary Manager

To open the Dictionary Manager, double-click on its icon in the Text-to-Speech group.

## Browsing

You can scroll through the list of words in the open dictionary with the up or down scroll keys on the right side of the Dictionary Contents box.

## Searching

You can find an entry by typing the word in the box marked English Word and clicking on the Find an Entry button. If the word is found, it's highlighted in the list at left. If not, you'll get a message.

## Adding

Add a new word to the dictionary by typing the word in the English Word box. Click on Insert Entry to add it to the active dictionary. You should test the entry's pronunciation before adding it.

## Testing

Click on Say English Word to hear how Monologue for Windows will pronounce it.

## Editing

You can change the way Monologue pronounces a word by typing the phonetic spelling in the Sound Like box. For that, you'll need to enter a "phonetic spelling"—a set of special characters that define sounds, or *phonemes*. You can also enter special characters, called *phoneme modifiers*, that change the pitch, speed or length of the sounds, to "fine-tune" the pronunciation.

## Deleting

You can remove words from the dictionary. To do so, use the Find Entry command to highlight the word, then click on the Delete Entry key.

## Saving a Dictionary

**Figure 7-13.**

Exception Dictionary
Save Dictionary File
As dialog

To keep your changes to the dictionary, click on Save Dictionary for the Save Dictionary File As dialog:

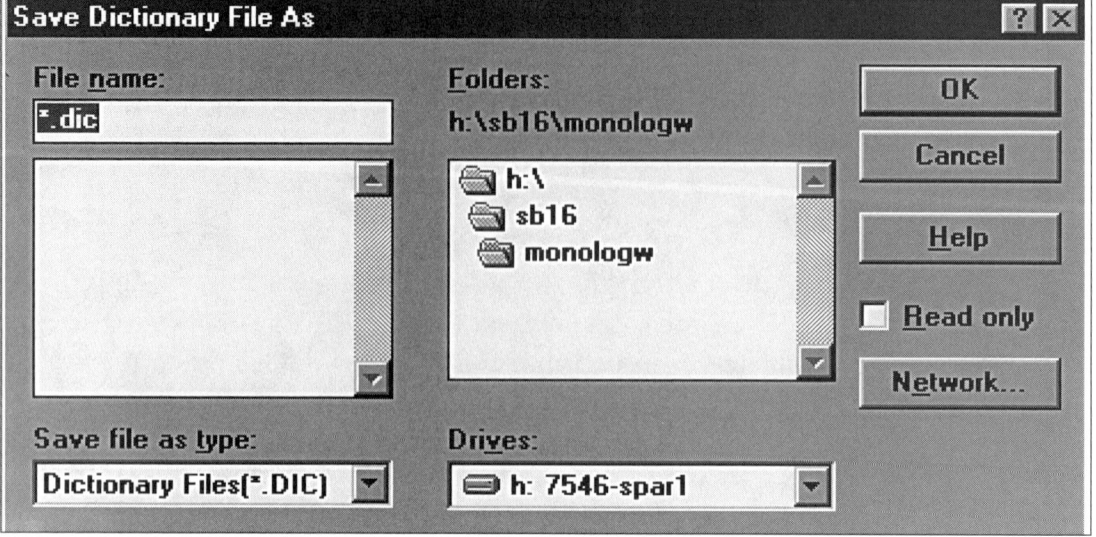

Type in the name of your new file and click on OK; if the file exists, thstem asks if you want to overwrite—the option is yours. The only file you can not replace Is KERNEL.DIC—that's Monologue's original dictionary that it requires.

## Choosing a Dictionary

Once you have saved your own custom dictionary, you can choose to make it active. Here's how:

**Figure 7-14.**

Exception Dictionary
Select Active
Dictionary File dialog

**1**   Click on Active Dictionary; this dialog box appears:

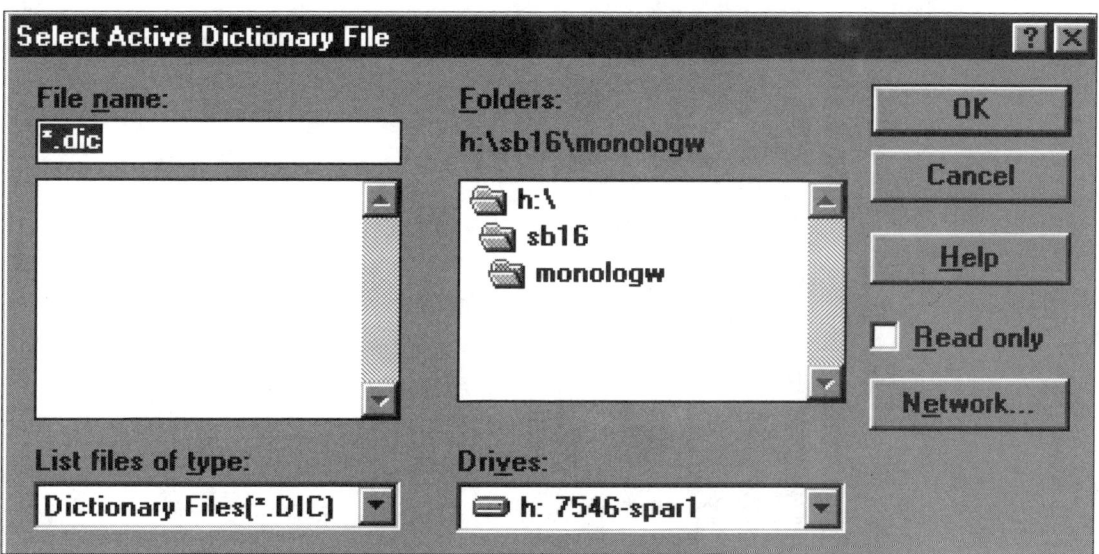

**2**   Click on the File Name of the dictionary file you want

**3**   If you do not want anyone to update the dictionary, click on Read Only

**4**   When you finish, click on OK

Click on the Open Dictionary button to select another dictionary to edit. You'll get this dialog box:

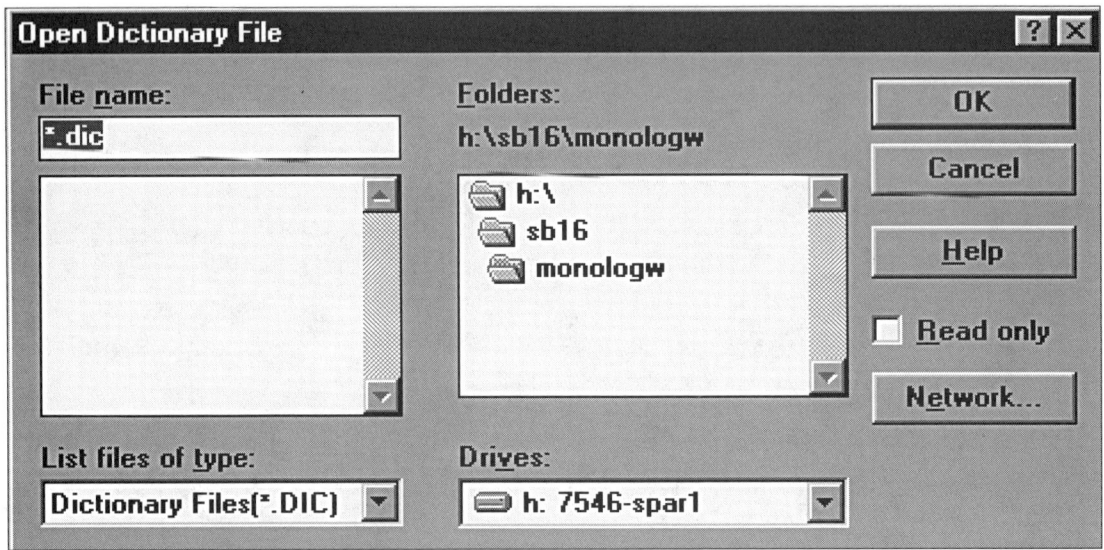

**Figure 7-15.**
Select Open
Dictionary File dialog

Highlight the name of the file you want, then click on OK.

*If you decide not to keep any changes you have made during an edit session, simply do not click on the Save Dictionary button. To continue using Monologue for Windows but with the unchanged dictionary, click on the Open Dictionary button and reopen the same file.*

## Common Problems

Table 7-5 describes ways to deal with some of the problems you may have when using Monologue for Windows.

Now you have a sound basis for using many Windows applications. (I just had to say that.)

These are the last of the Windows-based software provided by Creative Labs. Next is a series of DOS-based audio applications that have most of the same functions as the Window-based ones. Some are even graphical. If you need DOS applications, read on.

**Table 7-5.** Common Problems

| Symptom | Reason | Cure |
|---|---|---|
| PC won't speak, but system does not crash. | The volume is set too low. | Increase volume control on the Sound Blaster card. |
| Clicking noises. | Computer is too slow, perhaps a 386. | Free up some memory by closing any applications you're not using; minimize open programs to icons, which use less memory than open windows; clear (or save and close) the clipboard; turn off desktop wallpaper by opening Control Panel, clicking on Desktop, and choosing None under Wallpaper; check the swap file by clicking on Control Panel, 386-Enhanced Mode, Virtual memory, and set to Permanent. |
| Speaking stutters. | Minor memory problem. | Try closing and reopening Monologue for Windows; if that fails, try suggestions for correcting clicking noises. |

# DOS Audio Applications

**T**his chapter is a brief rundown of the Creative Labs DOS applications provided with Sound Blaster 16. These are not Windows applications, and don't have the complete graphical interface or ease-of-use that implies. But for lower-speed PC's, those without VGA graphic display systems or those lacking Windows, they give surprisingly good results. Some even give you a graphical user screen and mouse control!

# SB16SET: DOS Mixer Utility

The SB16SET utility is the DOS version of Creative Mixer. It allows you to control the Sound Blaster 16 mixer in DOS.

## Starting SB16SET

To see the SB16SET control screen, do this:

1  Type the letter of the hard drive containing the Sound Blaster DOS applications, for example: **D:** then Enter. Then type **CD** \Sound Blaster16 and Enter, so you can change to the Sound Blaster directory.

2  Type SB16SET to activate the SB16SET control screen (Figure 8-1).

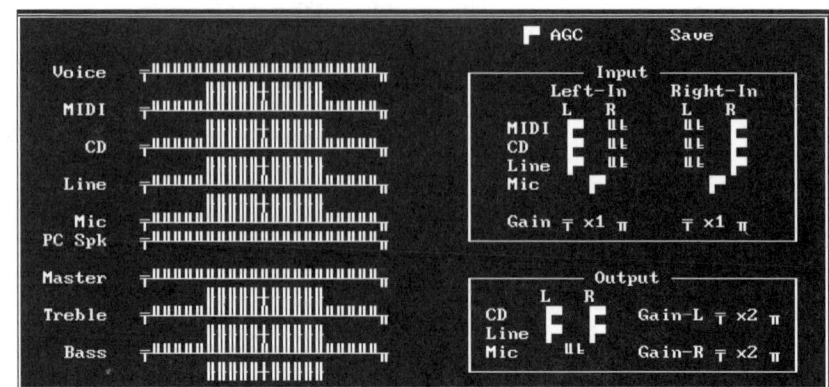

**Figure 8-1**
SB16SET DOS Control
Screen

# Using SB16SET

The components of the control screen let you adjust your input and output.

## Volume Control

Shown on the left side of the screen, the sliders control volume levels for every audio source. The Volume control is the larger, longer slider for each source. Audio sources are Voice, MIDI, CD, Line, Microphone, PC Speaker, Master, Treble, and Bass.

## Balance Control

Shown on the left side of the screen, the balance sliders control how much audio goes to the left and right speakers for stereo input. The balance control is the smaller, shorter slider for each source. Sliding to the left lowers volume for the right speaker, but the left speaker does not change. Sliding to the right lowers volume for the left speaker, but the right speaker does not change.

## Automatic Gain Control

Automatic Gain Control (AGC) sits atop the screen, just off center. Use this when recording from a microphone to automatically adjust input gain for a clear recording.

## Save

Click on the Save button to keep all your changes.

## Input

Use the Input box for two purposes:

 Select your audio input source for the mixer

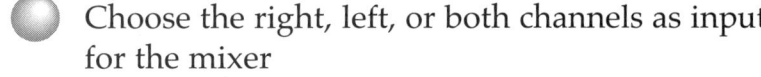 Choose the right, left, or both channels as input for the mixer

Your available sources are MIDI, CD player, Line, and Microphone. You must send channel input to its correct output channel. In other words, left-channel input must go to left-channel output; the same is true for the right channel. You can't swap channels in DOS the way you can in the Windows-based Creative WaveStudio.

Increase or decrease gain (volume level) of the audio source by clicking on the left/right arrow keys in the Input box.

## Output

Choose the input audio sources to control as output from the chosen input. Allowed inputs here are the Microphone In, CD, and Line In jack. Here, you can also adjust the volume level (gain) for the left and right channels.

## Moving Around the Mixer

You can use the mouse or the keyboard in SB16SET.

## Mouse control

● **Make your selection** by clicking on the box you want, placing an X in the box. To deselect, click on a box that already has an X in it.

● **Control the volume or balance** by clicking on a slider, holding down the right mouse button, and dragging the slider to its new spot.

● **Exit the mixer** by clicking on the box in the upper left corner.

## Keyboard control

● **Move forward** between control groups by pressing [Tab]

● **Move backward** between control groups by pressing [Shift]-[Tab]

● **Move between controls in a group** by pressing [↑] or [↓]

● **Adjust volume or gain** with [←] and [→]

● **Change a selected check box** by pressing [Spacebar] or [Enter]

● **Exit the mixer** by pressing [Esc]

# QuickCD: DOS CD Player

QuickCD is the DOS version of EnsembleCD; it lets you play audio CDs on your CD-ROM drive under DOS. This application has much the same features of the Windows version. When you start QuickCD, you'll see a CD player and mixer on screen.

## Starting QuickCD from DOS

Do this to turn on your DOS CD-audio player:

**1**   Change to the Sound Blaster 16 directory by typing **CD \SB16** and pressing [Enter]. Remember that if you assigned a different directory during installation, you'll need to change to that directory name.

**2**   Type **QCD** and press [Enter]. You'll see the QCD Control Panel (Figure 8-2 on pg. 156).

## The Control Panel

QuickCD's Control Panel has all the buttons that you'd expect on a high-end CD player, plus a few things that only a computer would need.

**Figure 8-2.**
QuickCD DOS control
panel

## Display Panel

Just as your regular stereo and the EnsembleCD panel, this panel (Figure 8-3) shows which track is playing, how long the track has been playing, and (for your PC only) the CD-ROM's drive letter.

**Figure 8-3.**
QuickCD display
panel

## Power Button

Click on the Power Button to turn off QuickCD.

## CD Eject Button

When you click on this button, the CD drive alternately opens (unloads) or closes (loads). It works for the standard single-platter CD-ROM drive only.

## Transport Control Buttons

Figure 8-4 on pg. 157 shows how these buttons control the CD in your drive. Table 8-1 gives the details.

**Figure 8-4.**
QuickCD transport
control buttons

**Table 8-1.** QuickCD Transport Controls

| Button | Description |
|--------|-------------|
| Stop | Stops playing the CD |
| Pause | Pauses or resumes playing the CD |
| Play | Plays the CD |
| Reverse | Repeats the current track of the CD |
| Fast Forward | Advances to the next track |
| Previous Track | Plays the previous track |
| Next Track | Plays the next track |

## Track Selector

The buttons in Figure 8-5, below, let you choose a track by number. For example, if you want to hear track number 7, click on the button numbered 7. To select a two-digit track number, like 12, press the "../.." button on the right side of the panel before clicking on the one and the two.

**Figure 8-5.**
QuickCD track
selector buttons

## Function Buttons

QuickCD uses graphic-covered buttons so you can choose and play several tracks for your listening pleasure.

Below, Figure 8-6 shows these controls and Table 8-2 on pg. 158 describes how they work.

**Figure 8-6.**
QuickCD function
buttons

**Table 8-2.** QuickCD Function Buttons

| Function | Description |
| --- | --- |
| Operating mode | *Normal* plays the 1CD from the first track to the last in order. |
| | *Random* plays the CD tracks in a different order each time. |
| | *Programmable* plays the CD in the order you choose. Program your set by entering each track number when asked and clicking on the Set button. When done, press Play to hear your arrangement. |
| | *Repeat Track* keeps playing the same song over and over and over.... |
| | *Repeat Disk* keeps playing the entire CD over and over and over.... |
| Confirm | Confirms your operating mode |
| Sampler | Plays ten seconds of each track on the CD |
| Cancel | Stops the current function, letting you make another selection. |
| Display | Shows credits and copyright notices for QuickCD. |
| Choose | Go to another CD-ROM drive (if installed), but won't stop playing current drive. |

## QuickCD Gain Controls

**Figure 8-7.**
QuickCd gain
multiplier controls

Figure 8-7 shows the controls that set amplification levels of the CD audio input. Amplification levels can be increased only by two, four, or eight times.

## Volume/Tone Controls

Figure 8-8 shows the controls that adjust the volume and tone of your microphone, master, and CD input sources.

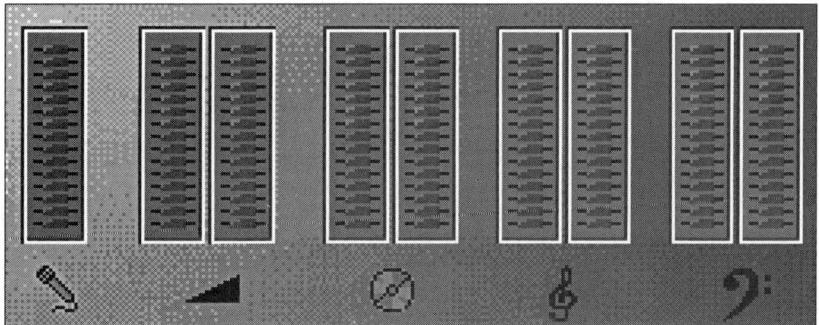

**Figure 8-8.**
QuickCD volume and
tone controls

## Channel Lock

This function locks the left and right channels so they increase or decrease together when you change the tone or volume settings. The small box atop the lock shows if the channels are locked or open (they are locked in the sample above this paragraph).

# QuickCD Mouse and Keyboard Commands

The mouse and keyboard can both be used to manipulate the QuickCD control panel.

## Mouse

Use the mouse to control QuickCD like this:

- **Increase or decrease volume or tone** by clicking on the indicator.

- **Increase to the maximum level** by clicking above the volume or tone indicator.

- **Decrease to the minimum level** by clicking below the volume or tone indicator.

# Keyboard

Table 8-3 explains how to run QuickCD from the keyboard.

**Table 8-3.** QuickCD Keyboard Commands

| This Command | Does This.... |
| --- | --- |
| Tab | Move to the next option |
| Shift-Tab | Move back an option |
| ↑/↓ | Increase volume, tone, or gain |
| Enter | Select an option (press a button) |
| Esc | Exit QuickCD |
| Alt-A | Preview each track on the CD (the Sampler function) |
| Alt-B | Choose bass tone level indicator |
| Alt-C | Choose CD volume level indicator |
| Alt-E | Choose additional CD-ROM drive |
| Alt-I | Display info about QuickCD |
| Alt-M | Choose master volume indicator |
| Alt-N | Cancel current selection and function |
| Alt-O | Toggle through all program modes |
| Alt-T | Choose microphone level indicator |
| Spacebar | Choose selected button |
| 0-9 | Choose a track from 0 to 9 |
| / | Set track selector to accept two-digit number |

## Exit QuickCD

There are two ways to quit QuickCD:

- Click on the Power button.
- Press Esc.

# Record: DOS Sound Recorder

This DOS program lets you record sound to a computer file. Save sound files in one of two formats:

- Creative Voice (.VOC)
- Microsoft Wave (.WAV)

Unlike the Windows recording utility, there is no graphic interface in the DOS Sound Recorder. Instead, you must type all your commands at the DOS prompt.

*When entering commands at a DOS prompt, type carefully! Typos can mean that the command won't run. Worse yet, the command may run and do something that you don't want!*

## Recording Sounds

Table 8-4 describes the elements you'll need to type at the prompt to record a .WAV or .VOC file. First, though, here's the syntax:

RECORD *filename* [/A:*xx*] [C:*xx*] [/M:*xx*] [/R:*xx*] [/S:*xx*] [/Q] [/H] [?]

*A sound recording creates a new file or replaces an existing file. Double-check your filename before proceeding to be sure that you don't replace a file you needed to keep! Also, the recording will stop when the disk is full, so be sure that you have plenty of disk space free for your file.*

**Table 8-4.** Recording Command Elements

| Option | Description |
|---|---|
| *filename* | The name of the file you will create; include the extension for a wave (.WAV) or voice (.VOC) file. |
| /A:*xx* | Selects input source (or multiple sources) with these abbreviations (in capital letters)[1] |
| C:*xx* | Selects compression format—enter ALAW, MULAW, or CTADPCM. |
| /M:*xx* | Selects recording mode by setting *xx* as either MONO or STEREO. Default is MONO. |
| /R:*xx* | Select sampling resolution by setting *xx* at 8 bits or 16 bits. Default is 8 bits. |
| /S:*xx* | Select sampling rate. The default is .WAV, 11025 Hz. Remember that bigger is better[2] |
| /Q | Does not display recording information. |
| /H or /? | Displays recording information; this is the default if not specified. |

[1] *xx* =   MIC  (Microphone)

CD  (Audio CD)

LINE  (Sound unit connected to Sound Blaster 16 card's Line In jack ,like a cassette player or phonograph)

FM  (Existing FM file)

[2] .VOC format:  *xx*=  5000 to 44100 Hz

.WAV format:  *xx*=  11025 Hz; 22050 Hz; or 44100 Hz

# Play: DOS Play Utility

The DOS Play program lets you play back audio CDs, and these sound file types: wave (.WAV), voice (.VOC), MIDI (.MID), and Creative Music (.CMF).

## Playing Audio CDs

As with the DOS recording utility, there is no graphic interface here. This means that you have to type all your commands at the DOS prompt. Table 8-5 analyzes the commands for you.

*Warning: When entering commands at a DOS prompt, type carefully. Typos can mean that the command won't run. Worse yet, the command may run and do something that you don't want!*

Here's the command syntax:

PLAY CD [/T:*xx*] [/Q] [/H] [/?]

**Table 8-5.** Play Audio CD Commands

| This Option | Does This.... |
| --- | --- |
| CD | Identifies the CD-ROM drive as the audio input source. |
| /T:*xx* | Selects the track to start playing first; replace *xx* with a track number. If you omit this option, you must type the letter P to begin playing the CD from track 1 to the end. |
| /Q | Suppresses the display of playback information while CD is playing. Otherwise, you see the current track, total tracks, and key menu. |
| /H or /? | Shows HELP for using the Play command |

## Playing Other Sound Files

You can play wave (.WAV), voice (.VOC), MIDI (.MID), and Creative Music (.CMF) files. Table 8-6 describes the commands you need. Use this syntax to play these file types:

PLAY *file1* [*file2*...] [/Q] [/H] [/?]

**Table 8-6.** Sound File Play Commands

| This Option | Does This.... |
|---|---|
| CD/T:*xx* | Plays a CD source beginning with the track number you type in place of *xx*. |
| *file1* | Holds the name of the first file to play. |
| *File2*... | Holds the name of each additional file to play in sequence. All files played together in this command must have the same extension; that is, all files must be the same type. For example, you can not mix .MID files and .VOC files in the playback command. |
| /Q | Suppresses display of playback information while CD is playing. Otherwise, you see the current track, total tracks, and key menu. |
| /H or /? | Shows HELP for using the Play command |

## Tips and Warnings

- A description for using PLAY appears if you type the command with no parameters.

- When you forget to use extensions, PLAY looks for any files with the supplied names.

If you list several file names without extensions, PLAY will play back only one file. The program searches for files in this order: .WAV, .VOC, .MID, and .CMF. It stops looking after finding the first file.

To play .CMF files, you must load the **SBFMDRV**.COM driver into memory before entering the PLAY command. Start the driver by changing to the Sound Blaster 16 directory and typing SBFMDRV.

Use wildcard characters to select a group of files for playback. For example, if you type **PLAY *.WAV** the system will play all .WAV files in the directory. If you type **PLAY MY?.WAV,** you'll hear all files with three-letter names where the first two letters are MY.

The asterisk must be in the filename section of the name, before the period. You can not use a wildcard for a file extension (instead of .WAV, for example).

To play MIDI files, you have to set the MIDI environment first. Table 8-7 explains the commands, which take the following command syntax:

SET MID=SYNTH:x MAP:y

**Table 8-7.** MIDI Playback Commands

| Option | | Description |
|--------|--------|-------------|
| SYNTH:*x* | *x* = 1 | Internal; synthesizer (default) |
| | 2 | MIDI port |
| MAP:*y* | *y* = G | General MIDI file format |
| | E | Extended MIDI file format (default) |
| | B | Basic MIDI file format |

# Playback Keyboard Controls

You can control your sound file from the keyboard. If you need a quick reference once you're working with PLAY, just start the program without the /Q switch. A command menu will appear on the screen.

## Audio CD Control Keys

Table 8-8 lists the keys that control playing an audio CD:

**Table 8-8.** Audio CD Keys

| Key | Description |
| --- | --- |
| C | Start playing the CD from current track |
| Esc | Stop play and quit program |
| F | Fast forward the current track |
| L | Play previous track |
| N | Play next track |
| P | Play current track |
| R | Rewind to beginning of current track |
| S | Stop playing the current track |
| Spacebar | Pause playback (press C to resume) |
| X | Exit PLAY |

# Wave (.WAV) File Keyboard Commands

Table 8-9 lists the keys that control playing wave files:

**Table 8-9.** Wave File Keys

| Key | Description |
| --- | --- |
| C | Resume playing the selected wave file |
| Esc | Stop play and quit program |
| N | Play next wave file |
| P | Play current wave file |
| Spacebar | Pause playback (press C to resume) |
| <or> and Enter | Select another file from the list and play it |

## Voice (.VOC) File Keyboard Commands

Table 8-10 lists the keys that control playing voice files:

**Table 8-10.** Voice File Command Keys

| Key | Description |
| --- | --- |
| B | Stop a repeated section of the file, continuing to next section |
| C | Resume play |
| Esc | Stop play and quit program |
| N | Play next file selected |
| P | Play current file |
| Spacebar | Pause playback (press C to resume) |
| <or> and Enter | Select another file from the list and play it |

## MIDI (.MID) File Keyboard Commands

Table 8-11 lists the keys that control playing MIDI files:

**Table 8-11.** MIDI File Command Keys

| Key | Description |
|---|---|
| C | Resume playing the selected file |
| Esc | Stop play and quit program |
| ↑ / ↓ | Replay sound in a higher or lower pitch |
| M | Switch to a different selection of instruments based on the MIDI mapper standards (Basic, General, or Extended) |
| N | Play next file selected |
| P | Play previous file |
| Spacebar | Pause playback (press C to resume) |
| ↑ / ↓ | Speed up or slow down tempo of the file |
| <or> and Enter | Select another file from the list and play it |

## Creative Voice (.VOC) File Keyboard Commands

Table 8-12 lists the keys that control playing voice files:

**Table 8-12.** Voice File Command Keys

| Key | Description |
|---|---|
| C | Resume playing the selected file |
| Esc | Stop play and quits program |
| ↑/↓ | Replay sound in a higher or lower pitch |
| N | Play next file selected |
| P | Play previous file |
| Spacebar | Pause playback (press C to resume) |
| <or> and Enter | Select another file from the list and play it |

# SBTALKER: DOS Text to Speech

The DOS Text to speech converter has essentially the same functions as Monologue for Windows. The DOS version reads ASCII text aloud through your Sound Blaster 16 card. Like Monologue for Windows, SBTALKER uses phonetic rules.

## Starting SBTALKER

To start SBTALKER:

**1**   Exit Windows.

**2**   Change directories to C:\SB16\SBTALKER (remember to replace C:\SB16 with your own drive and directory names if you did not use the default during installation).

**3**   Type **SBTALK**; press Enter.

## Expanded Memory

SBTALKER will load itself into expanded memory if you have specified an Expanded Memory Specification (EMS) driver. You install such a driver to allow SBTALK-ER to use available memory above the 640K DOS limit. This way, you can "read" and "speak" larger files.

If EMS drivers are already installed, you'll find these lines in your CONFIG.SYS file:

DEVICE=C:\DOS\HIMEM.SYS

DEVICE=C:\DOS\EMM386.EXE

## Add Echo

When starting SBTALKER, you can add an echo effect to any text read aloud. To set the echo effect, do this:

1    Type **SET-ECHO [*dddd*]**; replace *dddd* with the length of your echo-delay. For example, when *dddd*=1000 you have an echo delay of 1/10th of a second. A value of 500 causes a reverb effect.

2    Press [Enter].

## Removing SBTALKER

You need to remove SBTALKER from memory when you're done. Otherwise, it will remain in memory and limit the number of files you can open for other applications. To remove SBTALKER from memory, do this:

1    Change directories to C:\SB16\SBTALKER.

2    Type **REMOVE**; press [Enter].

# Reading Text

SBTALKER reads three types of input:

- ASCII text files
- Text reader
- DOS command input

## ASCII Text Files

To read ASCII text files, do this:

**1**    Type **READ > filename [/w]** at a DOS prompt,
replacing *filename* with the actual name of your
ASCII text file. (The /w option tells READ to
also display the text it is speaking.)

**2**    Press (Enter); SBTALKER reads the file aloud to
its end.

*Test this function by using a test file supplied by Creative
Labs, SBTEST.TXT:*

READ > SBTEST.TXT /w

## Reading from the Text Reader

Text Reader waits for you to type text. It reads aloud as
you type the words on screen. Use Text Reader like this:

**1**    From a DOS prompt, type **READ**.

**2**    Press (Enter).

**3**    Stop the program by pressing (Ctrl)-(Z) or
(Ctrl)-(C), then press (Enter).

## Reading from a DOS command

SBTALKER can read aloud a specific "string" of text from a DOS command. To read from a DOS command, do this:

**1**    At a DOS prompt, type **READ** *entered-text*, replacing *entered-text* with your own words.

**2**    Press [Enter]. The READ command causes SBTALKER to "say" the *entered-text*. For example, type:

READ this is your favorite DJ

The PC will say those words when you press [Enter].

# Intelligent Organ: DOS Piano

Intelligent Organ lets you use your keyboard as if it were an electronic organ. However, if you're really into creating music, hook up a MIDI keyboard to the Sound Blaster 16 MIDI interface instead; the keys work a *lot* better.

# Starting Intelligent Organ

To start Intelligent Organ, do this:

**1**    Change directories from a DOS prompt to C:\SB16\**PRO_ORG**, then press [Enter].

**2**    Type PRO_ORG, then press [Enter] to see the Intelligent Organ screen (Figure 8-9)

## Using the Keyboard

The Intelligent Organ keyboard has a seven-octave range. Each octave is lettered, A through G; the lowest octave is A, and the highest is G. Middle C is the first (lowest) note of the "base" octave: octave D. Two keyboard play modes are available:

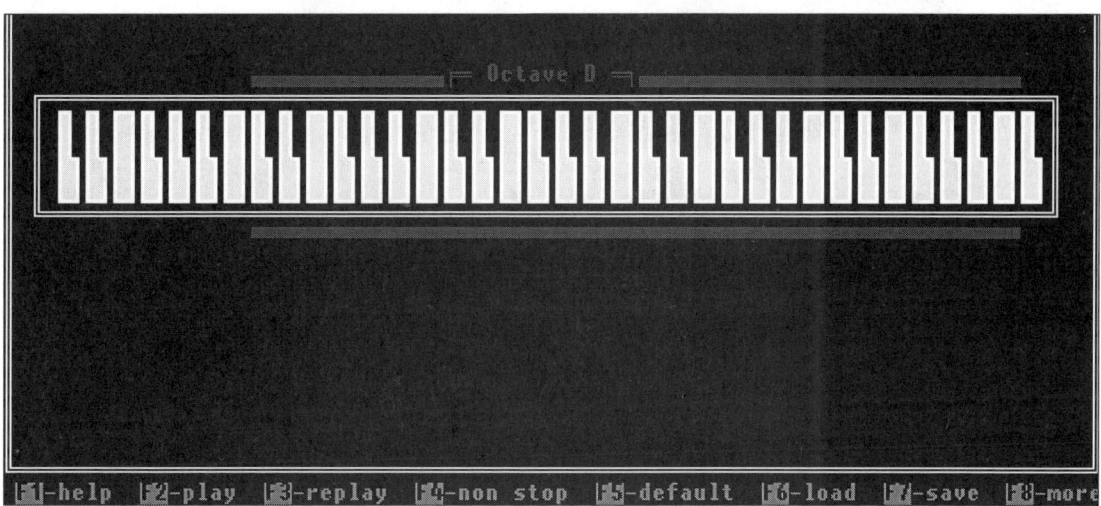

**Figure 8-9.**
Intelligent Organ
main screen

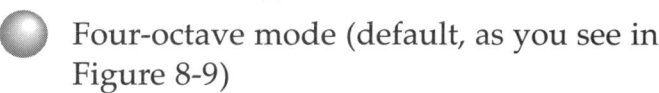 Four-octave mode (default, as you see in Figure 8-9)

Two-octave mode (not shown)

## Four-Octave Mode

Four-octave mode lets you use only the white keys of four currently chosen octaves. The heavy bars above and below the on-screen keyboard show which octaves are active. You can change the default octaves by pressing ⟵ and ⟶. You'll see the heavy bar slide left or right accordingly.

You play the notes by pressing keys on your PC's keyboard. Here are the letters to use in four-octave mode:

NOTES ("white" keys only)

| OCTAVE | C D E F G A B |
|--------|----------------|
| C | Z X C V B N M |
| D | A S D F G H J |
| E | Q W E R T Y U |
| F | 1 2 3 4 5 6 7 |

## Two-Octave Mode

Two-octave mode gives you access to both the white and black keys of the on-screen keyboard—but for only two octaves instead of four. Switch to two-octave mode by pressing Tab. You'll see the green bars shorten to cover just two octaves. The computer keys for the white keys appear on the graphical on-screen keyboard; computer keys for black keys appear below the keyboard. Here are the PC keyboard keys for the two octaves (black keys shown as flats):

| OCTAVE | C | Db | D | Eb | E | F | Gb | G | Ab | A | Bb | B |
|--------|---|----|---|----|---|---|----|---|----|---|----|---|
| | D | Z | S | X | D | C | V | G | B | H | N | J | M |
| | E | Q | 2 | W | 3 | E | R | 5 | T | 6 | Y | 7 | U |

As with four-octave mode, you can change the default octaves by pressing ← or →. You'll see the heavybar slide left or rightaccordingly.

## Learning to Play

Intelligent Organ has a built-in tutor. The tutor plays a song, showing which keys to press. To learn to play Intelligent Organ:

1   Press F6 for a list of prearranged songs to learn.

2   Select the song you want and press Enter. The song loads into your PC's memory.

3   Press F2 (Demo) to play the whole song.

4   Press F8 (More), then F1 (Learn). On your screen appears a "map" showing the standard PC keyboard with the corresponding notes.

■ 5    Press F2 to let Intelligent Organ teach you how
to play the song. Intelligent Organ will begin the
song, then prompt you to play along. As the
song plays, each on-screen key is highlighted to
indicate the next key you should play. If you
don't get to the key in cadence with the music,
Intelligent Organ stops and waits for you.

## Stop the Music

To cancel your lesson, press Esc.

## Intelligent Organ Settings

You can review or change the settings for Intelligent
Organ by doing this:

■ 1    Return to the main screen.

■ 2    Each time you play a prearranged song,
Intelligent Organ automatically changes the settings for instruments, key, tempo, scale, rhythm
and volume to suit the song. To return to the
defaults, do this:

   ⬤ Press F5

   ⬤ Type the letter O for Original settings

   ⬤ Press Enter

■ 3    Press F2 to play or review the settings;an on-
screen table appears showing the current settings, and any changes you make. Below, I've
described the keys you use to make these
changes.

When you begin playing, Intelligent Organ records
your performance, using the instrument and other settings you choose.

## Volume

Press Home to raise the volume, and press End to lower the volume.

## Key

Change the key of your composition by pressing + or ⎵.

## Instruments

Change instruments by pressing the function key of the instrument desired. There are five instruments assigned to each of function keys F1 through F4, for a total of 20. See Table 16-1 for the available Selections. Each key steps through its list of instruments, so you may have to press a key five times to select the instrument you want. To select an oboe, for example, press F3 twice.

**Table 8-13.** Instrument Choices

| [F1] | [F2] | [F3] | [F4] |
|---|---|---|---|
| Piano | Organ 1 | Violin | Synthesizer 1 |
| Harp | Trumpet | Oboe | Bass Synthesizer |
| Electric Guitar | Saxophone | Flute | Sitar |
| Marimba | Trombone | Harmonica | Javaican |
| Alien | Mars | Clarinet | Bells |

## Accompaniment

Add rhythmic accompaniment by pressing function keys F5 through F5. As with instruments, each function key has several rhythms, so you'll have to press a key several times for your choice.

## Arpeggio

An *arpeggio* is when the notes of a chord are played separately instead of together. To play an arpeggio:

**1**     Press a left or right square bracket ([ or ]) to select a numbered arpeggio. Keep pressing the bracket until the arpeggio desired appears.

**2**     Intelligent Organ plays your selection.

**3**     Use ↑ and ↓ to alter the volume of your arpeggio.

**4**     When you're done playing the selection, press the apostrophe.

## Saving a Song

Before saving a song, listen to it and make sure it's worth the disk space. To play a song from memory before saving to disk, do this:

**1**     Return to the Main menu by pressing Esc.

**2**     Press F4 to replay the song until you press Esc. *Do not press* F2 ! F2 clears the buffer and you will lose your changes.

To save the music from the buffer, do this:

**1**     Return to the Main menu by pressing Esc.

**2**     Press F7 for this message:
Enter organ file to save:

**3**     Type your new file name and press Enter.

**4**     When you're done, clear the buffer by pressing F2 .

## Replaying the Song

To load the selection, do this:

**1**    From the Main menu, press F6 for a list of available songs.

**2**    Highlight your selection, then press Enter.

Play the song by doing this:

**1**    Press F3 to play the song once.

**2**    Press F4 to play the song over and over until you press Esc.

# Changing Defaults (the ones used when you first run Intelligent Organ)

**1**    Return to Main menu if needed.

**2**    Press F5 for the Default Settings window; an on-screen list box appears

**3**    To return to the default title for Intelligent Organ, type the letter T and this text:

CMS's Intelligent Organ

**4**    To change the defaults for a single song instead, type **T** and the name of that song. When you finish changing settings for a song, save that song again.

**5**    Press Tab to the setting you will change, or press the letter that appears in red.

**6**    Press ← or → until the desired setting appears.

**7**   Switch all settings to defaults by pressing ⃞O
       (for Original).

**8**   When you finish, press ⃞Enter⃞.

## Exit Intelligent Organ

To exit Intelligent Organ, press ⃞F8⃞ (More), then ⃞F4⃞
(Quit). This request appears:

Exit to DOS (y/n)?

Press ⃞Y⃞.

# Installing Sound Blaster 16 and Creative Labs CD-ROM Drive

**Y**ou probably bought your Sound Blaster as part of a multi-media computer, didn't you? The card was already installed, and so were all the applications for it (the software) including a CD-ROM drive. Lucky you: you can skip this appendix–you don't need it!

But if you have a Sound Blaster 16 card and perhaps a CD-ROM drive and software that are not already installed, this appendix is for you! I'll show you how to install and set up these things and get you started enjoying some quality new sounds.

Here's what I cover in this appendix:

○ Installing the Sound Blaster 16 audio card

○ Installing the CD-ROM drive

○ Connecting the CD-ROM drive to the PC and the Sound Blaster 16

○ Connecting the PC internal speaker to the Sound Blaster

## Preparing to Install Sound Blaster Hardware

You'll need a small Phillips screwdriver (the cross-pointed kind) for most of the screws you'll discover to remove the computer cover and install the sound card and CD-ROM drive. You may also need a very small straight-bladed screwdriver to disconnect certain cables.

**1** If this is your first time opening up a computer, don't be too anxious about it. Adding stuff to the inside of a computer is really straightforward. It's not like being a space cadet; you don't even need special boots or a helmet! And, you'll get something out of it: the pleasure of doing it yourself, a chance to see what's inside that magic box, and the enjoyment of better sound. So, let's get to it!

# Installing the Sound Blaster 16 Audio Card

To install your new audio card, take the following steps:

**1** Turn off the computer, monitor, external modem, printer, and whatever else is attached to the power line.

**2** Disconnect the cables from the back of the PC. To remove the keyboard cable (and some others), simply pull them straight out of their sockets. Some other cables are attached with small screws on each edge; unscrew the screws and then pull the cable out. Other cables have "thumbscrews;" unscrew them with your fingers and then pull the cable out. (Be sure to remember where cables plug in. You might want to label each cable with a note marked on a bit of masking tape.)

**3** Place the PC on a large flat work surface that's clean, so you can work on it easily. You might cover the area with clean paper. It's not the most ecological, but the best covering to prevent static electricity is aluminum foil.

Whatever you do, don't use a plastic surface. (I'll discuss this more in a bit.)

**4**    Remove the PC's cover. Check your PC hardware manual for specifics on how to do this. Some covers are U-shaped, and surround the case at top and sides. Other covers may only fit on the top or one side. If you have a tower case with two side covers, you probably want to open up the one on the left side (as seen from the front panel).

Before starting, locate all the screws or plastic tabs that hold the cover in place. A word to the wary: many PC's have sheet metal parts inside that are very sharp. Be careful you don't cut yourself on the edges.

Slowly slide the cover from the computer. If the cover seems stuck, don't pull hard. Look for any more screws or plastic tabs that might be holding the cover down. When you're done, carefully set aside the screws holding the cover in a safe place.

**5**    Place the PC on the table so you can get to the boards inside. You'll be able to see all the cards for various devices that are already installed. IMPORTANT: Avoid touching anything inside the PC just yet.

Place your Sound Blaster 16 card next to the PC.

*Leave the card in its special shiny protective envelope for the moment; don't touch the card itself. Put your screwdrivers on the table next to you.*

**6**    For the following steps, you need to be sure there's no static electricity buildup that could damage your sound card or the PC itself. A single, almost invisible static spark could destroy your new investment. These precautions are even more important if you are live in a dry region or in an air-conditioned space.

First, sit down next to the table and don't move around. (Shuffling around on a carpet or handling plastic bags, for example, are great ways to create big static sparks.) Next, touch both the PC metal frame and the sound card envelope with your hands at the same time. (This gets rid of any existing static.) If you get up from the table, always touch the PC frame again when you return (to "ground" yourself).

I know this all sounds tedious and even a bit silly, but that's life in the static zone. A better and more convenient way to handle this is to wear an anti-static wrist strap, available for a few dollars in many PC retail shops. Follow their directions.

Now open the Sound Blaster 16's special anti-static envelope, remove the board and set it on top of the envelope.

It's time to decide on some options for the Sound Blaster 16 board. Because these options are selected directly on the board, you need to set them before you install the board. If you forget, you'll have to go through the whole process again.

Here are the options that can be set on the board:

⬤ The base I/O address

⬤ The MIDI port base I/O address

⬤ The joystick port enable

⬤ The audio output type

Don't panic–I'll explain everything. Just you wait. First, all these options are selected using "jumpers"–tiny connectors that slip onto pins mounted on the board. To install a jumper, you simply slip it over a pair of pins; to remove one, grasp it in your fingers (or using a pair of tweezers) and slide it off the pins.

(For you "techies" out there, the DMA and IRQ settings are not covered here because they're done in software, not by jumpers. I'll talk about them when we come to installing the software.)

**IMPORTANT**: Before you check or change jumpers, touch the PC's metal frame with one hand and the metal handle of the Sound Blaster card with the other hand. (Don't touch any other part of the card at this moment.) This dissipates any lingering static, and you can now handle the card safely.

**7**   The two first items to set are the electronic locations (the "addresses") your PC uses to "find" and "talk to" the Sound Blaster. Except in rare cases, the standard addresses already set in the card work just fine. The important thing is that the Sound Blaster addresses must be different from any other card installed in your PC (and they almost always are).

For the record, the standard base I/O address is 220H and the standard MIDI I/O address is 330H (the "H" stands for "hexadecimal," a number system used in PC's.) It's so unlikely you'll need to change these, you can probably forget all about them. (I already have.)

**8**   You'll want a joystick port on your PC of course–but only one of them! (A second port would be a conflict for your PC–and it's always good to avoid conflicts!) Your new Sound Blaster 16 has a joystick port ready to use. Problem is, your PC may already have a game card or some other card with a joystick port. If it does, you have two choices: remove the existing joystick port or disable the one on your Sound Blaster 16.

If you decide to disable the Sound Blaster joystick port, you'll need to change a jumper on the audio card.

## JUMPER JOYSTICKS

You already like your joystick plugged in just the way its is? Okay–but you'll have to disable the joystick function ("port") on your new Sound Blaster card. Here's how:

The factory "turns on" the Sound Blaster 16 joystick port by putting a jumper marked JYEN in place. You'll find that jumper near the center of the card–in the middle of a row of five jumpers. To "turn off" the Sound Blaster joystick port, remove jumper JYEN.

(Even when disabled in this way, the joystick port still functions as a MIDI port–for connection to MIDI keyboards, for example. Check out the MIDI section in Chapter 1.)

**9**     Finally, you need to decide about your audio amplifier output. You have two choices: power output (for speakers or headphones) or low-level output (for external amplifiers). The on-board power amplifier provides 4 watts per channel for 4ohm speakers or 2 watts for 8ohm speakers. It's plenty for small accessory speakers or for headphones, but not nearly enough for hi-fi speakers. And, distortion levels are quite high while frequency response is limited.

If you have a stereo amplifier available nearby, use it to get much better audio quality and much higher power. Connect the low-level outputs from the Sound Blaster output directly to preamp inputs on the amplifier–the kind of input you'd use for a tuner or tape deck.

Here's how to select this option: you'll find jumpers OPSL and OPSR on the board near the board handle (where all the external devices plug in). The regular setting is with the internal amplifier connected; OPSL and

OPSR are both connected to pins 2 and 3. To switch to low-level output (for an external amplifier), move both jumpers up to the opposite pins (pins 1 and 2). Now, the "speakers out" jack becomes a "line out" jack.

*Some versions of the Sound Blaster 16 (the "Value" edition for example) may not have these jumpers. Instead, they have both a speaker-out and a line-out jack. Simply use the output jack that suits your needs.*

**10**   Time to choose a "home" for your new Sound Blaster 16. You can put it only in a "16-bit" type slot on your PC's motherboard. (The motherboard is the main board of your computer–the one all the cards plug in to. A 16-bit slot has a much longer connector than an 8-bit slot. It's possible that your PC doesn't even have an 8-bit slot; in that case, any slot will do.)

Be sure that the slot you choose can accept both of the connector tabs on the bottom of the card (an 8-bit slot can only accept a board with one tab). If you have a choice, pick a slot with an empty slot on either side of it. That gives room for cables, and it also reduces the chance for unwanted electrical noises creeping from the computer to contaminate your new sound.

If this slot position doesn't currently have a card in it, there should be a thin metal plate covering the back opening of the PC. It has a little tab at the end that is held in place with a single screw. Hold onto the plate with one hand and remove the screw. Slide the strip straight out of the PC, and save the screw to hold in the sound card.

Here's your big moment: time to install the Sound Blaster 16 card (drum roll please).

**IMPORTANT**: To make sure there's no lingering static, touch the PC's metal frame with one hand and the metal handle of the Sound Blaster card with the other hand. (Don't touch any other part of the card at this moment.) Now you can safely handle or pick up the card.

Line up the card's metal handle with the opening at the back of the computer (where you removed the metal plate in the last step). Be sure that the gold-striped tabs on the bottom of the card line up with the 16-bit slot you selected. Press down firmly on the top edge of the card. You'll feel the card slide in place; the top of the metal bracket will line up with the screw hole on the opening at the back of the computer.

11 Screw the Sound Blaster's metal "handle" to the opening at the back of the computer; use the screw you saved from removing the blank plate. This screw is important: it holds the board securely in place and prevents it from getting dislodged when you plug cables into it.

If you've lost the screw (you didn't did you?), it may be a standard American type, or it just might have metric threads. Remove a spare screw and take this sample to the hardware store or your local PC repairman to find a match. If you can't find one, as a last-ditch solution, steal one from an empty slot to hold down the Sound Blaster. DON'T leave the board floating loose; if it falls out of its slot with the power on, it's almost certain to become mincemeat.

That's it for the Sound Blaster board! But hang in there: do you have a CD-ROM drive to install? If so, read on.

## Installing the Sound Blaster CD-ROM Drive

Your Sound Blaster CD-ROM needs a Sound Blaster 16 sound card to control it. If you haven't already installed one, go back and do that first. Also, if you installed a Sound Blaster in the past and are now about to add a CD-ROM, go back and review the steps about removing the PC's cover and taking precautions for static electricity. (Very important.)

*These instructions are for a Sound Blaster provided CD-ROM drive, typically made by Panasonic. Other drives with similar designs may work, but there's no guarantee they will. You'll need to read their included instruction guides to install them properly–especially when it comes to cable connections. You're on your own!*

*It's also possible to install a second CD-ROM drive to a Sound Blaster, but that's unusual, and beyond the scope of this book.*

## Installing the Sound Blaster CD-ROM drive

It's even easier to install the CD-ROM drive than the sound card. Here's how:

1   First, you'll need to clear the opening to a vacant drive bay. Your CD-ROM drive looks a lot like a 5.25-inch floppy disk drive (a "big" floppy–not the "small" 3.5-inch kind), and installs in the same size space, or "bay." (You do have a spare bay available, don't you?)

To open up your spare drive bay, you usually need to snap the blank plastic plate out of the front panel with a flat-head screwdriver.

Instead of using a screwdriver, try reaching behind the panel from inside the PC, put your finger in the center of the panel and pop it out the front. (In a few cases, you may first need to remove your PC's front panel by gently tugging around its edges with the computer cover removed.)

Once you've removed the blank panel, you may find a metal plate covering the opening. Like most things in a computer, this is probably secured with a Phillips screw. Remove the plate and set the screw aside–you'll probably need it later. Sometimes you'll find a "permanent" plate blocking the opening; you can usually bend it back and forth a few times until it breaks off.

**2** Time to install the CD-ROM drive! You probably have one of two types of mounting setups. The most common PC case simply has a bay with no space on either side; four screws hold the drive in the bay. The other kind of case requires two small "rails" on each side of the drive. (This is an old-fashioned system, but still in use.)

*To discover if you need to use rails, look at a floppy disk drive that's already installed. If that drive is not secured directly to the sides of the bay, you should see metal or plastic rails attached to the drive that slide in slots on the side of the bay–and that means you'll need 'em for the CD-ROM drive, too.*

If your PC case needs rails, be sure to screw the rails onto the drive before you try to install it. Then simply slide the drive in place onto the slots in the case. If you don't have any rails, you'll need to find some at your favorite computer store.

**3**    Gently slide the drive from the front into the open drive bay. Be sure the top of the drive is toward the top of the PC case. (The door to insert the CD is at the top edge of the drive, and the controls are along the bottom edge.) Secure the drive to the bay using screws in the places shown in the little drawing that came with your drive. (Of course it did!)

It's time to connect the wires and cables from the Sound Blaster CD-ROM to the computer's power supply and the Sound Blaster 16 audio card.

# Connecting the CD-ROM to the Sound Blaster 16 and PC

The Sound Blaster 16 card controls the Sound Blaster

CD-ROM drive. The CD-ROM has three connections:

● Data cable to audio card (flat strip)

● Audio cable to audio card (thin wire)

● DC power plug from the PC power supply (thick wires)

Locate the data cable and audio cable in the Sound Blaster packing box; find the power supply inside the computer. The data cable is the wide, flat cable with a bar at either end containing its connections.

4 Plug the data cable into the CD-ROM drive.
The cable plugs in to the drive only one way,
and has a colored stripe to help you align it.
You can't plug it in wrong without forcing it;
keep the colored strip toward the right side of
the drive (as viewed from the rear). Push the
connector bar straight into the drive connector
(about 1/4-inch) until it stops.

Connect the data cable to the CD-ROM drive with its
colored stripe toward the right side of the drive (as seen
from the rear).

*Notice the colored stripe along one edge of the data cable. Keep
this stripe on the right edge of the cable as it plugs into the
CD-ROM drive (when viewed from the rear).*

5 Plug the audio cable into the CD-ROM; it plugs
into the right side of the drive (as seen from the
rear), and is shaped so it will only easily plug
in one way.

6 Plug in a spare dc power cable from the
computer power supply to the CD-ROM. To
locate the power supply, look for a rectangular
metal box that has a fan in it, mounted on the
back panel of your PC. The dc power cables are
hanging from a hole in this box, draped into the
PC. You should find a spare cable hanging from
the power supply and not plugged into
anything else.

*The dc power connector is a plastic bar with four tube-like
holes on its end (hooked to the wires from the power supply).
Simply plug the connector into the drive on the left edge (as
seen from the rear); you may have to wiggle it gently to get
it all the way in. (Notice that the bar has tapered edges, so it
can only easily plug into the CD-ROM drive in one direc-
tion. The tapered edge goes to the bottom edge of the socket*

*on the CD-ROM. Be very careful to match the shape of the bar to the shape of the socket on the drive.) Be sure not to bend the little pins when you plug in. (Some power supply cables may have another kind of connector: a tiny 4-pin bar meant for 3.5-inch floppy drives; you can't use that cable–look for another spare one.)*

**7** Connect the data and audio cables to the Sound Blaster 16 card. For the Sound Blaster card, keep the colored stripe of the data cable at the top edge of the card (the edge farthest from the motherboard). There is a notch on the audio cable that should also face up.

# Connecting the Internal PC speaker to the Sound Blaster

Follow these simple steps to allow the Sound Blaster 16 card to control the internal PC speaker:

**1** Locate the speaker in your PC and find the twisted pair of wires that connect it to the PC motherboard. Unplug the small plug that connects these wires to the motherboard.

**2** Locate the two tiny pins near the top edge of the Sound Blaster marked PC SPK. Plug the speaker connector onto these pins.

**3** In some cases, the PC speaker connector is four pins wide, but only one pin on each end is used. With care, you can remove one wire and its tiny connector spring and put it back in a hole in the connector next to the other wire. You can now plug in one end (two pins) of the connector to the pins on the Sound Blaster. (It doesn't matter which wire connects to which pin.)

After this change, you can adjust all your system sounds, including those assigned to your Windows startup and exit sequences. That's a real help at two in the morning when the baby's sleeping, or at 3p.m. when your office-mate is sleeping!

After all the installation, take a good look around inside the PC! Check to see that all cables and connections to floppy drives and the hard drive are still secure. Sometimes it's hard to see if one of the flat bar connectors on a data cable has loosened up; just push it firmly into the drive (or into the controller card connector) with your thumb until it stops moving. If you dislodge a cable connection to a floppy drive, you may get this error message when you turn on the computer:

FDD SEEK FAILURE

Or, if there's a hard-drive cable loose, you might get a message like:

DRIVE NOT READY

In this case, the PC will want to boot from the floppy drive. If so, you'll have to open the computer again and re-connect the offending cables. A little patience checking first can save you a lot of irritation later on.

**4**    Carefully slide or set the cover back on the PC. Tighten the screws on the cover (don't overdo it). Then reconnect the monitor, keyboard, mouse, and other cables. (Now you'll be glad you put those labels on!) Plug in the ac power cables to the computer and other devices.

Congratulations! Your Sound Blaster 16 and CD-ROM drive are ready to be tickled into life by some software applications. Read Appendix B to learn how to install this software and test your sound setup.

# Installing Sound Blaster 16 Software

**R**eady to start listening to those new quality sounds? Well, almost ready. You'll need to install the basic driver software and then the applications that operate your new Sound Blaster 16. Briefly, here are the steps:

- Install the diskette-based software that sets up the drivers that allow your PC to use the CD-ROM drive.

- Using the CD-ROM software, install the Sound Blaster drivers and application software (including Windows-based software).

- Test the Sound Blaster card for proper sound generation.

This appendix describes each of those steps. It's probably a good time to point out that Microsoft Windows should be installed on your PC. Although the regular Sound Blaster software package also includes a set of DOS applications, its Windows-based applications are more complete and easy to use–and lots more fun!

If you have a pre-loaded multi-media PC bundle, it is just about certain to have Microsoft Windows already installed.

If you're about to install Windows for the first time, I strongly suggest you choose Windows for Workgroups version 3.11 instead of "plain" Windows. It's a more reliable product and it's noticeably faster; the price is only $10 or $20 more than the "plain" version. (Unless you have a need for network features, simply tell the Windows for Workgroups Install program you don't want them. That will save disk space, and speed up Windows a tad more.)

On the other hand, now that Windows 95 is widely available, you may want to install that instead. I strongly urge you to use the CD-ROM version of Windows 95 instead of the monster pile of diskettes you'd otherwise have to wade through. (This means you'll first need to install the required DOS CD-ROM drivers in your CONFIG.SYS and AUTOEXEC.BAT.)

*Special note about Windows 95: I installed a Sound Blaster 16 using its own drivers, and with its Windows applications running in Microsoft Windows 95. (Many of the illustrations in this book show Windows 95 screens.) Windows 95 includes built-in Sound Blaster drivers, and you should probably use them instead of the ones included with the Creative Labs installation software. Windows 95 will automatically "seek out" your new Sound Blaster and install the right drivers.*

*I did have some problems running the Sound Blaster speech applications in Windows 95 (and I did not test the DOS applications). If you have similar problems, contact Creative Labs for new versions of these products that may work more reliably.*

In Chapter 1, I discussed audio input and output devices and how to install them. But all you really need for testing your installation is a pair of stereo headphones or a small pair of speakers to listen to the Sound Blaster's audio output. (Use headphones or speakers with the common 1/8-inch ("mini") stereo plugs–or pick up an adapter.)

# Before You Start

Before you use any software provided on floppy disks, it's a good idea to make backup copies of the originals. Use only the backups for installation and set the originals aside in a safe place. Here's how to make those copies:

**1**    Begin by "write-protecting" each of the diskettes you're copying. Slide the little black tab at the corner of each diskette so the square hole is open.

**2**    Find some blank 3.5-inch high-density diskettes. "Write-unprotect" each of them by sliding the little black tab so the square hole is closed (you can't see through it). If these diskettes aren't blank, or your're not sure, you should format each of them before the next step. At a DOS prompt, type FORMAT A: (assuming A: is the letter of your 3.5-inch floppy drive. After that, DOS will prompt you to insert each diskette (one diskette at a time, please).

**3**    Now, copy each diskette:

At a DOS prompt, type COPY A: A: (assuming A: is the letter of your 3.5-inch floppy drive). DOS will prompt you to put the original floppy in the drive, will "read in" its contents, and will then ask you to insert the blank diskette to copy to. Repeat this for all diskettes in the package.

**4**    Now hide the original diskettes in a safe place where you can never find them again!

Special note about Windows 95: I installed a Sound Blaster 16 using its own drivers, and with its Windows applications running in Microsoft Windows 95.

Windows 95 includes built-in Sound Blaster drivers, and you should probably use them instead of the ones provided by the Creative Labs installation software. More on that later.

Before you begin installation, you should find out what your boot drive is and in what drive and directory your Microsoft Windows is installed in. (You'll be asked these questions as part of the installation process.) Your boot drive is where your PC starts up in, using DOS; it's almost always drive "C". Microsoft Windows is usually installed in the "C:\WINDOWS" directory, but may be in another drive, such as "D". (Note the quotes are not part of the drive and directory designation.)

# CD-ROM Software

Creative Lab's Sound Blaster 16 Software CD-ROM disk provides the quickest and most efficient means to install all your software at one time. It contains all the required drivers, and all the applications I've discussed here. It also has a slick graphical installer that prompts you for any options.

(It even contains a copy of the software that's usually provided on floppy diskettes. If you need diskettes, but don't have them, or if you have a bad one, you can make copies from the CD-ROM. More on that later.)

But there's a small glitch: at first, your PC doesn't even know how to use the CD-ROM drive. To "teach" it, you need to install software from a floppy that loads a QuickCD program and drivers needed for your CD-ROM. Follow these steps to install the drivers and software:

1  Place the CD-ROM Installation Disk (CR563) into your 3.5-inch floppy disk drive. (This is the diskette that gets your PC ready to use the CD-ROM drive; it's not a CD-ROM disk.)

**2** At a DOS prompt, type either A: or B: (whichever identifies your 3.5-inch floppy disk drive), then press the [Enter] key.

**3** Type INSTALL, then press [Enter]. Follow the directions to install the CD-ROM drivers. You'll be prompted when to re-boot your PC and insert the CD-ROM disk.

To start your CD-ROM installation disk, you may need to run the program stored on it. Verify which drive letter is assigned to your CD-ROM; it's usually the next drive after your hard-drive. For example, if your last hard drive is "C", your CD-ROM should be "D".

I suggest you run this CD-ROM installation from DOS, not from a DOS prompt in Windows. No other programs should be running. To start, type D:INSTALL (assuming that "D" is your CD-ROM). When you start, you'll be in a 'windows-like' graphical menu system, running in DOS. Here's what you'll see and enter:

**1** First, you'll be asked which language you wish to use during install: English/French/German/ Italian/Spanish. When you choose one of these, the following prompts and message will be in that language.

**2** Next, select the base I/O address for your Sound Blaster 16 board. (Unless you've had to change the jumpers, as described in Appendix A, accept the default: 220.) The installation software will verify that your Sound Blaster is installed with this address.

**3** A welcome screen appears, and you should first choose [F2] to view the Readme file, then press [Enter]. Read this document to see if any recent changes to the Sound Blaster 16 product affect your installation. When you're done reading, exit the document viewer.

**4** Choose Begin Installation and press [Enter]. You'll be asked for a Full or Custom installation. If you are installing to Windows, I suggest you select Custom and then choose not to install the DOS applications.

**5** You'll be asked to verify you want the files to be loaded into a "C:\SB16" directory. I suggest you put the files in the same directory you have Windows installed in. If that's drive C, accept the directory suggested; otherwise, you'll want to change the drive letter. (It's a good idea to accept the standard "SB16" directory; if it doesn't exist already, the installation will create it.)

**6** You'll be asked to verify your "boot drive" as C. (That's the drive your PC starts running DOS on.) C is almost always the correct choice.

**7** You'll be asked to verify various other settings:

| | |
|---|---:|
| Base address | 220 |
| MIDI address | 330 |
| IRQ (Interrupt request) | 5 |
| DMA low | 1 |
| DMA high. | 5 |

The default settings I've shown here are almost always correct. (In a few cases, an IRQ of 5 may conflict with a bus mouse, or a printer port, and you'll need to change it. In that case, try using an IRQ of 10. But remember, you'll first need to remove the card and change jumpers, as I described in Appendix A, then re-start the installation.)

**8**   The CD-ROM now proceeds to chug away for a
few minutes, loading all the sofware you've
selected, and making a few other changes.

**9**   The installation stops, and informs you what
changes it's made to the CONFIG.SYS and
AUTOEXEC.BAT files. If you do find major
problems with this installation, you can start
over using the backed-up (un-modified) versions of these files.

**10**   If you have chosen to install the Windows
applications (in Step 4),you'll be asked to verify
the Windows path so that it can install the
required Windows drivers. Usually (but not
always) the path is C:\WINDOWS. The CD will
now install these drivers. (If you're using
Windows 95, I suggest you skip installing any
drivers from this CD that replace the ones in
Windows 95. That's because the Windows 95
versions are newer and more compatible.)

**11**   Finally, the install screen will let you "exit to
DOS" or "re-boot." If you want to start using
the Sound Blaster and its applications, you
must re-boot your PC to load the drivers and
configuration software. (If you want to wait
until later, and simply return to DOS now, you
can do that instead.)

*Typically, the installation program adds these lines to your
CONFIG.SYS file:*

```
    DEVICE=C:\SB16\DRV\CTSSB16.SYS/UNIT=0
/BLASTER=A:220 I:5 D:1 H:5
    DEVICE=C:\SB16\DRV\CTMMSYS.SYS
    FILES=40 (only if your CONFIG.SYS had no FILES=
line, or one that that was less than 40)
    It also adds these lines to your AUTOEXEC.BAT file:

SET BLASTER=A220 I5 D1 H5 P330 T6
SET SOUND=C:\SB16
SET MIDI=SYNTH:1 MAP:E
C:\SB16\DIAGNOSE /S
C:\SB16\SBSET /P
```

*In case you need to revert to the original files, the system saves them with the extension .B~K. For example, the old C:\AUTOEXEC.BAT becomes C:\AUTOEXEC.B~K. Once the installation is successful and everything works okay, you may want to get rid of these useless files. At the DOS prompt, type C:, then press enter, then type cd \ then press enter, finally type del \*.b~k, and press* Enter.

# Windows Applications

If you're adding a CD-ROM drive to a system that already has Windows, you need to add the MCI CD Audio driver now. This driver lets you use the CD drive for playing music while you're at the computer.

## Drivers

Without the MCI CD Audio driver, you will receive the following error message when starting Windows with the CD-ROM installed.

A configuration or hardware problem has occurred. Use the Drivers option in the Control Panel to reconfigure the Sound Blaster Drive.

To correct this error, you need to go to the Control Panel and install the needed drivers. That is, double-click on the Control Panel icon (in the Main Program Group):

The Drivers icon in the Control Panel Group looks like this:

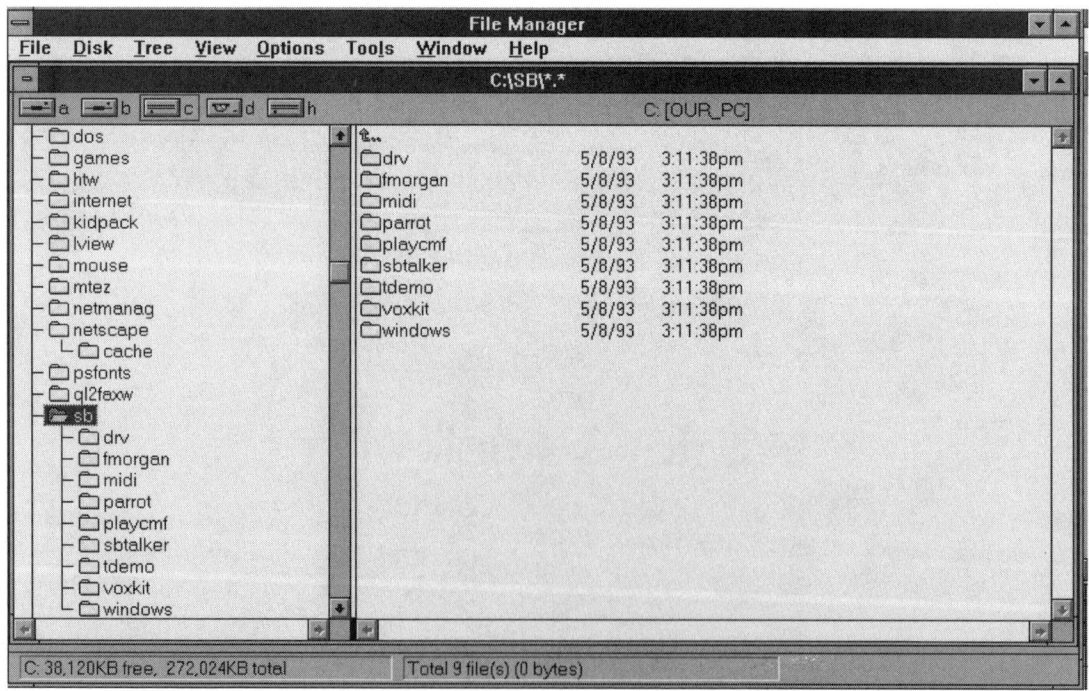

**Figure B-1**

```
C:\SB>del *.*
All files in directory will be deleted!
Are you sure (Y/N)?Y_
```

**Figure B-2**

## Installing the MCI CD Audio Driver

Here are the steps to follow to get the audio driver working:

**11** Double-click on the Drivers icon for a list of installed drivers. The set of drivers you get includes all those needed to use the Sound Blaster CD-ROM and audio card. The one needed for CD-ROM is the one named MCI CD Audio. If this is on your list of installed drivers, you can play audio CDs on the CD-ROM drive with no further effort. If it's not on the list, continue.

**2** To add MCI CD Audio, click on the Add button.

**3** Scroll through the list of drivers until you find the one named MCI CD Audio. Click on this driver name, then click on OK.

**4** The driver should be in C:\WINDOWS\ SYSTEM (if you want to look for it, the file name is MCICDA.DRV). If not, you will be asked to type in the name of the directory where the file is stored.

**5**   After you find the driver, click on OK to add the driver.

Now your driver list should be updated with the MCI CD Audio driver.

## Installing CD-ROM Drivers

These two drivers control the CD-ROM drive:

● SBCD.SYS  The device driver for the CD-ROM drive

● MSCDEX.EXE  The Microsoft CD-ROM Extensions program

The CD-ROM installation program automatically edits your computer's CONFIG.SYS file to include a line like this:

DEVICE=C:\SB16\DRV\SBCD.SYS  /D:MSCD001 /P:220

Your AUTOEXEC.BAT file picks up this line:

C:\SB16\DRV\MSCDEX.EXE /D:MSC001 /V /M:15

## What Do the SBCD.SYS Settings Mean?

Some of the SBCD.SYS settings allow for options, if needed. You may edit a setting (called a parameter) with any ASCII text editor, like the MS-DOS Editor or even Windows Write. Here is the syntax of the SBCD.SYS line in the CONFIG.SYS file:

DEVICE=C:\SB16\DRV\SBCD.SYS  /D:device-name
/P:xxx [/N:x] /S:[mode][ID] [/a] [/x:1]

**Table B–1**  SBCD.SYS Settings

| Parameter | Description |
| --- | --- |
| /D:device-name | The CD-ROM drive name, which must be the same as the CD-ROM drive name in the AUTOEXEC.BAT file. The default is /D:MSCD001. |
| /P:xxx | The Sound Blaster 16 base address. The default is 220, but xxx can be 220, 240, 260, or 280. In the rare case that some other equipment is already using 220, you'll need to select another address. If you do, you'll also need to remove the Sound Blaster card to make jumper changes. |
| /N:x | Shows the number of CD-ROMs installed. Values of x can be 1, 2, 3. |
| /S:[mode][ID] | mode tells the speed of your CD-ROM. |

**A –Automatic** Transfer speed varies with the type of disk. A data disk's transfer speed is 300Kb (kilobytes) per second. A CD with data and audio, called mixed mode, has a transfer speed of 150Kb per second.

**N –Normal** Transfer speed is 150Kb per second (a "single-speed" drive).

**D –Double-speed** Transfer speed is 300Kb per second (this is the default: a "double-speed" drive).

ID shows the drive's identification number. Values are 1, 2, or 3, for up to three separate CD-ROM drive connections. If you don't specify ID, the mode setting applies to all drives. For example, /S:N shows that all connected drives are in normal mode. When you specify ID, the mode value applies only to the drive indicated by the ID, so that /S:A2 shows that drive number 2 depends on the type of disk for its transfer speed (A mode).

**Table B-2**

| Parameter | Description |
| --- | --- |
| /A | Sends sound to both channels (stereo-style) even if the program sends it to one channel (mono-style). |
| /X:1 | Stops an error message if software eject is unavailable. Use it only when you have CD-ROM models 521 or 523 as the first drive in a daisy-chained sequence. |

# What Do the MSCDEX.EXE Settings Mean?

The syntax of the MSCDEX.EXE line in your AUTOEXEC.BAT file follows:

C:\SB16\DRV\MSCDEX.EXE
/D:device-name /L:drive-letter [/E]
[/M:xx] [/V] [/S]

## Table B-3  MSCDEX.EXE Settings

| Parameter | Description |
| --- | --- |
| /D:device-name | The same CD-ROM drive name used in the SBCD.SYS line of the CONFIG.SYS file. The default is /D:MSCD001. |
| /L:drive-letter | Drive letter assigned to the CD-ROM drive. If not specified, the next drive letter is used. For example, if your hard drive is C, then the CD-ROM drive will be D. |
| /E | Specifies use of Expanded Memory when available; applies only to Expanded Memory Manager LIM (Lotus-Intel-Microsoft) version 3.2 or later. |
| /M:xx | Sets the number of buffers for temporary storage of recently accessed data. xx ranges from 2 to 30. Each buffer uses about 2K of RAM, so assigning too many buffers may hinder programs with large memory needs. |

CONTINUED ON PAGE 212

CONTINUED FROM PAGE 211

**Table B-3  MSCDEX.EXE Settings**

| Parameter | Description |
|---|---|
| /V | Displays summary of RAM and expanded memory when computer boots. |
| /S | Allows CD-ROM drives to be shared on networked file servers (MS-NET only). |

## Changing the Speed Mode of Your CD-ROM

Changing the speed mode of your CD-ROM drive requires that you update SBCD.SYS. The program SETUPCD updates SBCD.SYS.

*Be sure that the drivers SBCD.SYS and MSCDEX.EXE are located in the Sound Blaster directory (SB16). If they're not, run the installation program again.*

Here are the steps to change the speed mode:

1   Change directories to the Sound Blaster directory; unless you specified something else during installation, type CD \SB16.

2   Type SETUPCD and press (Enter). Follow the on-screen directions for the CD-ROM Drive Setup. To quit at any time, press (Esc).

3   Choose the base I/O address for the Sound Blaster 16 and the speed mode for each drive.

The base address for a Sound Blaster 16 may be 220, 240, 260, or 280; the default is 220. The speed mode may be either A (automatic), N (normal), or D (double-speed); the Sound Blaster 16 default is D.

**4** When the system asks which drive the computer boots from, enter the drive letter (usually C).

**5** Reboot the computer to activate the changes.

SETUPCD saves the changes from step 3 in your computer's CONFIG.SYS file. The line added looks something like this:

DEVICE=C:\SB16\DRV\SBCD.SYS /D:device-name /P:xxx [/N:x] /S:[mode][ID] [/a] [/x:1]

You can change it later, if needed, by using an ASCII text editor.

# Deleting Older Versions of Sound Blaster

If you are replacing an older Sound Blaster product, there are two things you'll want to do:

● Delete any old files and directories of Sound Blaster files. Look for directories named SB or SBPRO.

● Remove old Sound Blaster commands from the AUTOEXEC.BAT file.

## Deleting the Windows Files

⬤ Open File Manager

⬤ Highlight the old Sound Blaster directory

⬤ Press ⌈Del⌋, click on OK, then click on Yes To All.

See Figure B–1 on page 206 for an old Sound Blaster directory (in Windows File Manager).

## Deleting the files using DOS

First, verify where the old Sound Blaster files are, for example, in C:\SB or C:\SBPRO. If you have a version of DOS that's 5.0 or newer, all you need to do is type DELTREE C:\SB or DELTREE C:\SBPRO to remove all the files and the directories at one time. If you have an older version of DOS, you'll want to follow these steps:

⬤ Change directory (for example, type CD \SB)

⬤ Type DEL *.*

⬤ Type Y (after you're sure you're deleting the files in the right directory–see Figure B–2).

See Figure B–2 on page 207 for a Delete old Sound Blaster files with DOS DEL

⬤ Show how many other subdirectories exist under the old Sound Blaster directory by typing DIR/W (see Figure B–3).

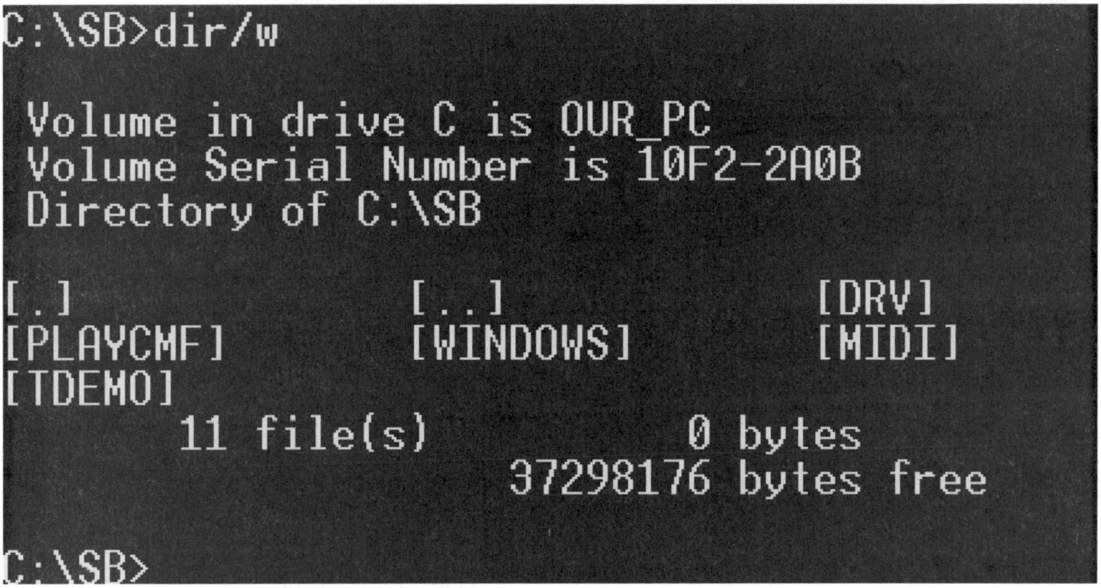

```
C:\SB>dir/w

 Volume in drive C is OUR_PC
 Volume Serial Number is 10F2-2A0B
 Directory of C:\SB

[.]                    [..]                   [DRV]
[PLAYCMF]              [WINDOWS]              [MIDI]
[TDEMO]
        11 file(s)                 0 bytes
                        37298176 bytes free

C:\SB>
```

**Figure B-3**

An old Sound
Blaster directory tree

- For each subdirectory, type DEL dir-name; for example, DEL DRV.

- To remove the subdirectory name, type RD dir-name; for example, RD DRV.

- When you finish, return to the root directory by typing CD \

- Remove the old Sound Blaster directory by typing RD dir-name (like RD SBPRO).

## Cleaning Up AUTOEXEC.BAT

Using a text editor, remove any lines in the AUTOEXEC.BAT file referring to the old directory. Two samples of old lines from an 8-bit SB card to remove follow:

SET BLASTER=A220 I7 D1 T3
@SET SOUND=C:\SB

A line to remove from an old Sound Blaster Pro installation may look like this:

C:\SBPRO\SBP-SET /M:12 /VOC:12
/CD:12 /MIDI:12

# Installing Sound Blaster 16 Software

The final step in your installation of the Sound Blaster card and CD-ROM is to install the DOS and Windows programs. (Of course, if you've used the CD-ROM version of the software, all installation is automatic.) The three installation disks do this:

● Create subdirectories for the audio card files under the SB16 directory (created when you installed the CD-ROM software). If you skipped the CD-ROM program installation, one of the disks creates the SB16 directory now. You'll have to go back later and add the CD-ROM files, though (unless you have another maker's CD-ROM drive).

● Copy the Sound Blaster 16 software and programs into the SB16 directories

● Copy the AUTOEXEC.BAT and CONFIG.SYS files into AUTOEXEC.B~K and CONFIG.B~K, then add new command lines to the AUTOEXEC.BAT and CONFIG.SYS files

● Add new lines to Windows INI files

*Before installing the Sound Blaster software, be sure to disable any disk-caching program like SMARTDRV or PC-CACHE. To do this, use a text editor and place a remark command (REM) before the line in your AUTOEXEC.BAT file. You must reboot to have the change take effect. Once you've successfully installed the Sound Blaster 16 software, you can take out the REM command to re-enable the disk-caching program.*

*The line you'll want to Remark-out looks like this:*

*C:\DOS\SMARTDRV.EXE 1024 /q /r*

Here are the steps for this simple installation:

**1** Insert the Sound Blaster 16 installation disk in your disk drive.

**2** If you are in WINDOWS or OS/2, exit and return to DOS. From the DOS prompt of your root directory (usually C:>) type A:INSTALL or B:INSTALL, depending on which drive is your 3.5-inch drive. Press (Enter).

**3** Four options appear on screen:

● See README file, press (F2)

● Begin installation, press (Enter)

● Learn about the installation process, press (F1)

● Quit installation, press (F3)

**4** I suggest you press (F2) now to check the README file for any recent changes to the installation that may affect your computer or operation system. Press (Esc) when you finish, to return to the main menu.

**5**   At the main menu, press (Enter) and follow the directions on screen. There are two installation options:

● Full installation

● Custom Installation

If you have the required 4 Mb of hard disk space, I recommend you select Full installation. Custom installation is a better choice if you have limited disk space or you want to choose which applications to load.

**6**   Confirm the name of the Sound Blaster 16 directory when the system asks for it–it should be C:\SB16, unless you specified something else during the installation earlier.

**7**   Press (Enter) to confirm the default settings for

*To learn if the default settings of the jumpers on the audio card are okay for your computer, you will run the test program DIAGNOSE, when these steps are complete.*

**8**   Give the system the Windows directory name when it asks for it–probably C:\WINDOWS, though you may have a different drive or directory name. For example, if your drive is double-spaced, the drive letter may be D. Some folks use a special name for their Windows directory, like WIN31. If you're not sure, exit the install process and use the DOS DIR command to find the Windows directory name. After typing the directory name, press (Enter).

**9**   When the installation process is done, reboot the computer by pressing(F10).

When the installation is finished, these lines appear in your AUTOEXEC.BAT file:

```
SET BLASTER=A220 D1 I5 H5 P330 T6
SET SOUND=C:\SB16
SET MIDI=SYNTH:1 MAP:E
C:\SB16\ DIAGNOSE /E
C:SB16\SB16SET /P
```

SET SOUND points to the directory where Sound Blaster 16 drives are stored. SET BLASTER sets hardware settings. The DIAGNOSE command starts the program to control the card's settings. The final line sets default volume settings for master, voice, CD audio, and MIDI (FM) music.

These lines appear in your CONFIG.SYS file:

```
DEVICE=C:\SB16\DRV\CTSB16.SYS
 /UNIT=0 /BLASTER=A:220 I:5 D:1 H:5
C:\SB16\DRV\CTMMSYS.SYS
C:\SB16\DRV\SBCD.SYS /D:MSCD001 /P:220
FILES=40
```

The program only adds the FILES line if you don't already have one, or if the existing FILES= statement has a number less than 40.

# Testing

Here's the payoff: now you've installed all this software, it's time to make sure it all works. The Sound Blaster 16 Diagnostic Utility tests to see that the card doesn't conflict with other hardware installed on your PC and that it can reproduce music and sound correctly. If the utility finds any problems, you can use it to update system files with the correct settings. Quit the test at any time by pressing F4 .

The computer may halt ("lock up") if another card is using the address you selected for the audio card (even if it's the Sound Blaster default). If this happens, shut off the PC and change the jumper settings on the sound card. (See the discussion on jumper settings and installing the Sound Blaster, in Appendix A.)

## Testing the Sound Blaster 16

Here are the steps to make sure everything is working properly:

**1** Return to the DOS prompt, which may mean leaving Windows or OS/2. From the DOS prompt (usually C:>), switch to the Sound Blaster directory by typing CD \SB16 (or use the directory name you specified during installation).

**2** Type DIAGNOSE and press [Enter] to begin the test program.

**3** Read the on-screen directions for the test program. Press [Enter] to begin. The utility will test the IRQ, Low DMA and High DMA channel settings.

**4** When the test has confirmed all settings as accurate, you will see the following information across the top of the test screen:

● I/O address  Default 220

● MIDI address  Default 330

● IRQ setting  Default 5

● DMA channels  Defaults 1 and 5

**5** Next, you get to test the audio function of your card and speakers. You test the left and right channels together (stereo), the left channel alone, and the right channel alone. Each test is run for 8-bit sound, 16-bit sound, and FM-synthesized sound.

*If you don't hear any sound, do this:*

*First, check to make sure that speakers are plugged in (sounds silly, but worth a quick check anyway).*

*Second, try using a pair of stereo headphones (with a mini-plug) instead of the speakers. (Don't plug the headphones into the CD-ROM drive; you'll only hear the sound from an audio CD if it's playing, not the audio from the Sound Blaster card.)*

*Third, try the stuff suggested in the section titled "I Can't Hear You–Solutions to Problems" later in this Appendix.*

## Testing the CD-ROM Drive

This test makes sure that the CD-ROM drive works. To run the test:

**1** Press the Eject button on the face of the CD-ROM drive. Place an audio CD in the drive. Close the drive by either pressing the Eject button again, or by gently pushing the CD caddy forward.

**2** From the DOS prompt, change to the Sound Blaster directory, which should be SB16 (unless you specified something else during the installation).

**3** Follow the on-screen guide.

The test will confirm two things:

● The drive is properly installed and set up. If an error occurs on the MSCDEX, there are two possible faults. One is that the data and power cables are not connected properly to the CD-ROM drive. Another is that the SBCD.SYS file is not loaded correctly.

● There is audio output. If you can't hear anything, even though the volume control is working and there is no MSCDEX error, look at the checklist in the next section.

## I Can't Hear You–
## Solutions to Problems

When there is no sound coming from your speakers, check these things before you panic:

● Speakers or headphones are securely plugged into the jack.

● Volume control on the speakers or CD-ROM is turned up.

● Volume control on Creative Mixer Windows application is turned up (see Chapter 3).

● External amplifier is correctly connected to the Sound Blaster 16. Be sure that the amp is turned on and that speaker or headphone connections are secure.

● Powered speakers have their power turned off if they are connected directly to the Sound Blaster 16 built-in amplifier.

If the FM music test and the audio CD work okay, but the 8-bit and 16-bit sound tests fail, this indicates the interrupt or DMA channel settings may be wrong. In this case, you may need to change jumper settings for these items, as I discussed in Appendix A.

# Installing Windows Applications

The system installs the Sound Blaster Windows group and icons when you first enter Windows after installing the Sound Blaster 16 software.

## Installing the Sound Blaster 16 Group

Here are the basic steps—about as easy as anything gets!

**1**    At the DOS prompt (usually C:>), start Windows by typing WIN and pressing Enter.

**2**    Once in Windows, you will see a message that says, "This program sets up the Sound Blaster 16 program group window." Click on OK. You will have a program group with icons for each application, looking something like this:

**Figure B–4.**
Sound Blaster 16 Windows program group

You may also have a second program group called Text-to-Speech, if you've installed these applications.

## Drivers and Applications

If you install Windows after installing Sound Blaster 16 files and programs, you'll need to add the Sound Blaster drivers and applications to your system yourself instead of taking advantage of the automatic Windows program group creation.

Here are the steps for adding Sound Blaster drivers and applications:

**1** Start Windows by typing WIN at the DOS prompt.

**2** From the Windows Program Manager, click on File, then click on Run. The Run pop-up window appears.

**3** Type C:\SB16\INSTALL. If you specified a different drive or directory during installation process and can't remember the name, click on the Browse button to search for the location of your Sound Blaster programs. When you've found the drive and directory, click on OK. The following illustration shows the Run pop-up window being used to add the Sound Blaster 16 drivers and applications under Windows:

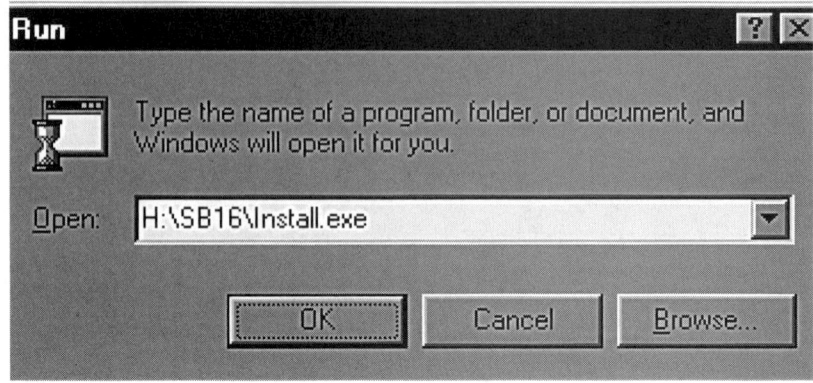

**Figure B–5.**
Windows 95
RUN pop-up

If your AUTOEXEC.BAT does not have the proper lines to start the SOUND and BLASTER drivers, INSTALL may not install the drivers and applications. You may need to return to a DOS prompt and type SET to confirm the settings before running INSTALL. (See the section earlier in this appendix titled "Installing Sound Blaster 16 Software on Your Hard Drive".)

Deleting duplicate icons is easy: just click on an icon and press Del, or click on File, Delete. When the system asks, "Are you sure you want to delete the item...," click on Yes to delete or No to cancel the command.

Click on the Sound Blaster Configuration icon in the Sound Blaster 16 program group, to change the Windows drivers settings when you change jumpers on the audio card or choose new IRQ or DMA settings. That icon looks like this:

**Figure B–6.**
Sound Blaster
Configuration
icon (Windows 95
shortcut)

The Sound Blaster Configuration dialog updates the AUTOEXEC.BAT, CONFIG.SYS, and SYSTEM.INI files. Changes only take place after you exit Windows and reboot the computer.

Congrats! Now you've finished the installation, and can move on to actually playing with this stuff. The next step is to attach audio and perhaps MIDI devices to the Sound Blaster card. To discover how, go back to the beginning of this book: read Chapter 1!

# INDEX

## A

## B

## C

# D

# E

# F

# G

# H

# I

# O

# P

# Q

# Available Now!

| | |
|---|---:|
| 1-2-3 for Windows: The Visual Learning Guide | $19.95 |
| ACT! 2.0: The Visual Learning Guide | $19.95 |
| The CD-ROM Revolution | $24.95 |
| CompuServe Information Manager for Windows: | |
| The Complete Membership Kit & Handbook (with two 3$^1$/2" disks) | $29.95 |
| Computers Don't Byte | $7.95 |
| Computer Gamer's Survival Guide | $19.95 |
| CorelDRAW! 4 Revealed! | $24.95 |
| CorelDRAW! 4 for Windows By Example (with 3$^1$/2" disk) | $34.95 |
| CorelDRAW! 5 Revealed! | $24.95 |
| Create Wealth with Quicken | $19.95 |
| Cruising America Online: The Visual Learning Guide | $19.95 |
| Excel 5 for Windows By Example (with 3$^1$/2" disk) | $29.95 |
| Excel 5 for Windows: The Visual Learning Guide | $19.95 |
| Excel for the Mac: The Visual Learning Guide | $19.95 |
| Free Electronic Networks | $24.95 |
| WINDOWS Magazine Presents: Freelance Graphics for Windows: | |
| The Art of Presentation | $27.95 |
| Harvard Graphics for Windows: The Art of Presentation | $27.95 |
| Internet After Hours | $19.95 |
| Internet for Windows—America Online Edition: | |
| The Visual Learning Guide | $19.95 |
| KidWare: The Parent's Guide to Software for Children | $14.95 |
| Lotus Notes 3 Revealed! | $24.95 |
| LotusWorks 3: Everything You Need to Know | $24.95 |
| Mac Tips and Tricks | $14.95 |
| Making Movies with Your PC | $24.95 |
| Microsoft Office in Concert | $24.95 |
| Microsoft Office in Concert, Professional Edition | $27.95 |
| Microsoft Works for Windows By Example | $24.95 |

| | |
|---|---|
| OS/2 WARP: Easy Installation Guide | $12.95 |
| PageMaker 5 for the Mac: Everything You Need to Know | $24.95 |
| PageMaker 5 for Windows: Everything You Need to Know | $19.95 |
| A Parent's Guide to Video Games | $12.95 |
| PC DOS 6.2: Everything You Need to Know | $24.95 |
| PowerPoint: The Visual Learning Guide | $19.95 |
| WINDOWS Magazine Presents: | |
| The Power of Windows and DOS Together, Second Edition | $24.95 |
| Quicken for Windows: The Visual Learning Guide | $19.95 |
| Quicken 3 for Windows: The Visual Learning Guide | $19.95 |
| QuickTime: Making Movies with Your Macintosh, Second Edition | $27.95 |
| The Slightly Skewed Computer Dictionary | $8.95 |
| Smalltalk Programming for Windows (with 3$^1$/2" disk) | $39.95 |
| Software: What's Hot! What's Not! | $16.95 |
| Superbase Revealed! | $29.95 |
| SuperPaint 3: Everything You Need to Know | $24.95 |
| Think THINK C! (with two 3$^1$/2" disks) | $39.95 |
| Visual Basic for Applications Revealed! | $27.95 |
| The Warp Book: | |
| Your Definitive Guide to Installing and Using OS/2 v3 | $24.95 |
| Windows 3.1: The Visual Learning Guide | $19.95 |
| WinFax PRO 4: The Visual Learning Guide | $19.95 |
| Word for Windows 2: The Visual Learning Guide | $19.95 |
| Word for Windows 6: The Visual Learning Guide | $19.95 |
| WordPerfect 6 for DOS By Example | $24.95 |
| WordPerfect 6 for DOS: How Do I . . .? | $24.95 |
| WordPerfect 6 for DOS: The Visual Learning Guide | $19.95 |
| WordPerfect 6 for Windows By Example | $29.95 |
| WordPerfect 6 for Windows: How Do I...? | $24.95 |
| WordPerfect 6 for Windows: The Visual Learning Guide | $19.95 |

# FILL IN AND MAIL TODAY

PRIMA PUBLISHING
P.O. BOX 1260BK
ROCKLIN, CA 95677

USE YOUR VISA/MC AND ORDER BY PHONE:
(916) 632-4400 (M-F 9:00-4:00 PST)

Please send me the following titles:

| Quantity | Title | Amount |
|---|---|---|
| _____ | _____ | _____ |
| _____ | _____ | _____ |
| _____ | _____ | _____ |
| _____ | _____ | _____ |
| _____ | _____ | _____ |

Subtotal         $_____
Postage & Handling
*($4.00 for the first book*
*plus $1.00 each additional book)*    $ _____
Sales Tax
*7.25% Sales Tax (California only)*
*8.25% Sales Tax (Tennessee only)*
*5.00% Sales Tax (Maryland only)*
*7.00% General Service Tax (Canada)*    $_____
TOTAL *(U.S. funds only)*    $_____

❏ Check enclosed for $_____(payable to Prima Publishing)
    Charge my   ❏ Master Card   ❏ Visa

Account No. _____Exp. Date _____

Signature _____

Your Name _____

Address _____

City/State/Zip _____

Daytime Telephone _____

Satisfaction is guaranteed— or your money back!
Please allow three to four weeks for delivery.
THANK YOU FOR YOUR ORDER